early years
wishing well

Collected rhymes, stories, songs and information text

Colours
and shapes

Author	**Editor**	**Designer**
Liz Powlay	Clare Miller	Rachael Hammond
Compilers	**Assistant Editor**	**Illustrations**
Stories, rhymes and information text compiled by Jackie Andrews	Saveria Mezzana	Jenny Tulip
Songs compiled by Peter Morrell	**Series Designer** Anna Oliwa	**Cover artwork** Alex Aylitte

Acknowledgement:
Qualifications and Curriculum Authority for the use of extracts from the QCA/DfEE document *Curriculum guidance for the foundation stage* © 2000 Qualifications and Curriculum Authority.

The publishers gratefully acknowledge permission to reproduce the following copyright material:

Jackie Andrews for 'The wonderful coat of colours' and 'What's in the parcel?' © 2001 Jackie Andrews, both previously unpublished; **Barbara Ball** for 'The Russian doll' © 2001 Barbara Ball, previously unpublished; **Clive Barnwell** for 'Little green man' © 2001 Clive Barnwell, previously unpublished; **Ann Bryant** for 'Food colours' and 'The shape song' © 2001 Ann Bryant, both previously unpublished; **Sue Cowling** for 'The shell' © 2001 Sue Cowling, previously unpublished; **Susan Eames** for 'If peas were red' and 'Just the same' © 2001 Susan Eames, both previously unpublished; **Barbara Garrad** for 'Favourite colours' © 2001 Barbara Garrad, previously unpublished; **Val Jeans-Jakobsson** for 'Jack and the balloon picture' © 2001 Val Jeans-Jakobsson; **Karen King** for

'The farm', 'A day at the fair' and 'The collage' © 2001 Karen King, all previously unpublished; **Johanne Levy** for 'Sky is so blue' and 'A great big square' © 2001 Johanne Levy, both previously unpublished; **Tony Mitton** for 'Creature colours' and 'Triangles' © 2001 Tony Mitton, both previously unpublished; **Julia Moffatt** for 'The perfect picture' © 2001 Julia Moffatt, previously unpublished; **Davey Moore** for 'Chocolate choice' © 2001 Davey Moore, previously unpublished; **Peter Morrell** for 'Black and blue!', 'Camouflage, camouflage' and 'Boxes' © 2001 Peter Morrell, all previously unpublished; **Sue Nicholls** for 'White' and 'Look for circles' © 2001 Sue Nicholls, both previously unpublished; **Jan Pollard** for 'Colour magic', 'Hair colours' and 'Tidying up' © 2001 Jan

Pollard, all previously unpublished; **Hazel Priestley-Hobbs** for 'Patterns' © 2001 Hazel Priestley-Hobbs, previously unpublished; **Geraldine Taylor** for 'Serena's favourite colour' and 'My finger puppet' © 2001 Geraldine Taylor, both previously unpublished; **Brenda Williams** for 'Colours here and colours there', 'Look at shapes', 'Painting patterns', 'Shape that dough' and 'Drawing shapes' © 2001 Brenda Williams, all previously unpublished; **Irene Yates** for 'The special day' © 2001 Irene Yates, previously unpublished.

Every effort has been made to trace copyright holders and the publishers apologize for any inadvertent omissions.

Text © 2001 Liz Powlay
© 2001 Scholastic Ltd

Designed using Adobe Pagemaker

Published by Scholastic Ltd, Villiers House, Clarendon Avenue, Leamington Spa, Warwickshire CV32 5PR
Printed by Ebenezer Baylis & Son Ltd, Worcester
Visit our website at www.scholastic.co.uk

1 2 3 4 5 6 7 8 9 0   1 2 3 4 5 6 7 8 9 0

British Library Cataloguing-in-Publication Data A catalogue record for this book is available from the British Library.

ISBN 0 439 01830 7

The right of Liz Powlay to be identified as the author of this work has been asserted by her in accordance with the Copyright, Designs and Patents Act 1988.

Contents

Early years wishing well: Colours and shapes

Contents

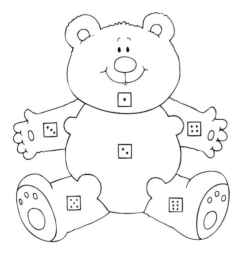

Early years wishing well: Colours and shapes

Wishing Well: Colours and shapes

The *Wishing Well* series is designed to help early years practitioners by suggesting exciting ways for them to provide a balanced curriculum for young children. The book contains a wealth of rhymes, stories and songs, linked to a familiar theme, and also offers information text and ideas to stimulate activities which meet the requirements of the Early Learning Goals.

Themes

Colours and shapes are a part of everyday life. Young children are surrounded by them at home and in their wider environment from the day they are born. By using themes that are within the child's recent experience, practitioners can build upon what is already known, and learning becomes relevant, integrated and fun. The activities suggested encourage this approach, helping children to develop a deeper understanding of the colours and shapes they see.

Using an anthology

Everyone enjoys stories, rhymes, songs and poems and an anthology is an interesting and stimulating way to extend and develop a child's learning. Young children benefit from the group participation that these texts encourage, as well as from the rhyme and repetition offered by poems and the melody of songs. The activities will help children to think about what is read to them, encouraging them to ask questions and seek further information.

Early Learning Goals

In meeting the demands of the Early Learning Goals and providing a balance of learning opportunities, practitioners may often find that time is limited. This book is therefore organized to provide quick and easy access to a range of original ideas. Users can be confident that all the activities closely relate to the requirements of the Early Learning Goals. The ideas can be applied equally well to the documents on pre-school education published for Scotland, Wales and Northern Ireland.

How to use this book

This book can be dipped into for a one-off session, or used to plan a mini topic or a whole theme. The majority of the activities encourage learning through a hands-on, play-orientated or conversational approach, as these are the ways young children learn best.

Start by browsing through the book and selecting texts and activities, using the children's interests, attention span and individual learning pace as a guide. Since the activities are related to a common theme, additional material from other pages can extend learning or provide opportunities for reinforcement.

The activities use easily obtained, inexpensive resources, with photocopiable pages providing further resources and support.

NB Throughout the book, several of the activities feature the use of food. Always ensure that you check for allergies and dietary requirements in these instances.

Colour magic

Red and blue make purple,
Yellow and blue make green,
Red and yellow make orange,
The loveliest colours you've seen.

Paint them on your paper.
Fold it and press it flat.
It makes a beautiful butterfly.
Now what do you think of that!

Jan Pollard

Early years wishing well: Colours and shapes

Colour magic

Personal, social and emotional development

★ Give pairs of children roller or squeezy bottles containing yellow and blue paint and encourage them to paint criss-crossing lines on a large sheet of paper. Point out where the paint mixes and makes green.

★ Ask the children to paint a picture in their favourite mixed colour to share at circle time.

★ Put red and blue paint in a zip-lock bag. Pass it around and notice the colours mixing.

Communication, language and literacy

★ Introduce the saying, 'As flat as a pancake'. Create sayings using similar starter phrases, for example 'As smooth as a…'.

★ Ask the children to write their names with felt-tipped pens on kitchen roll. Drip on water and describe the changes.

Mathematical development

★ Measure one drop of both yellow and blue food colourings into several clear jars. Add one tablespoon of water to the first jar, two to the second one and so on, and arrange the jars, near light, by water level. Encourage the children to describe the different shades.

★ Provide colour-change felt-tipped pens and ask pairs of children to write out numbers for their partners to trace over.

★ In the role-play area, set up a shop mixing and selling paint colours. Provide paint, water, spoons, tubs, money, pens and paper. Encourage the children to measure carefully, record their 'recipes' and buy the paints.

Knowledge and understanding of the world

★ Float drops of marbling ink in two colours on warm water. Stir the water gently and 'catch' the colours by laying a piece of paper on the surface of the water.

★ Make red and blue ice cubes. Invite the children to watch the pool of water as they melt and discuss the new colour.

★ Pour milk into a wide bowl. Drip on food colouring followed by washing up liquid. Watch the magical moving colours.

Physical development

★ Encourage the children to put red paint on a thumb and yellow on the first finger of the same hand and then to print tiny butterfly wings. Renew paint, rub together and print orange wings. Add features when dry.

★ Invite the children to place their bare feet in coloured paint and to walk across sheets of paper to make footprint patterns.

Creative development

★ Invite the children to paint on one wing of butterfly-shaped paper and, while the paint is wet, to fold the butterfly in half and press it flat.

★ Paint a mixture of two tablespoons of icing sugar and one of water onto paper. Drip food colouring onto the mixture and observe the way colour spreads.

Colours here and colours there

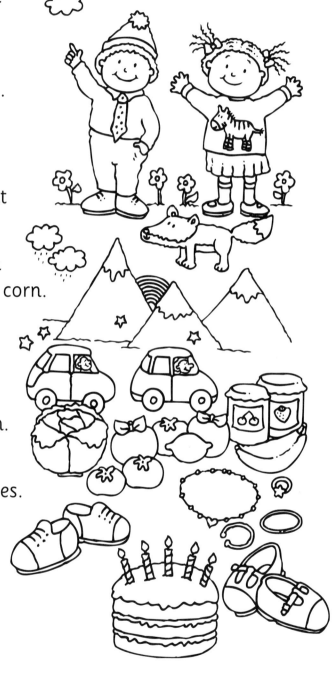

Colours here and colours there
Colours are just everywhere.

Purple hat, dark red tie
Yellow flowers, bright blue sky.

Orange sweater, scarlet socks
Stripy zebra, light brown fox.

After showers a rainbow bright
Multicoloured, shining light.

Speckled shadows on the lawn
Grey-green mountains, golden corn.

Silver cars and silver stars
Shiny fruits and jam in jars.

Red tomatoes, cabbage green
Jewellery with an amber sheen.

Patterned seas of many blues
Black and brown or pastel shoes.

Coloured candles on the cake
Light reflected on a lake.

Look around and you will see
Every colour there can be.

Brenda Williams

Colours here and colours there

Personal, social and emotional development

★ Paint the inside of shoeboxes in different colours and turn them onto their side to make open shelves. Ask the children to bring in items that match the colours and share a story about them before placing them in the boxes.

★ Put squares of colour from paint colour charts in a bag. Pass it around a circle and invite the children to take turns to pull squares out of it and match them to a selection of coloured objects in the middle of the circle.

Communication, language and literacy

★ Help the children to make alphabet star-viewers. Pre-draw letters onto pieces of black paper and make small holes with a cocktail stick along them. Tape each piece of paper onto a tube with the letter facing the inside. Invite the children to hold the tubes up to the light to see the letters.

★ Think of rhymes for different colours and clap the rhythm: 'red bed', 'green queen', and so on.

Mathematical development

★ Paint the inside of egg-boxes with a different colour in each compartment. Use them for sorting small coloured items.

★ Make a set of yellow flowers with one to five card petals and lolly-stick stems. Fill plant pots with play dough, and number them 1 to 5. Ask the children to 'plant' the flowers corresponding with each pot's number.

★ Ask the children to roll a dice, count the spots and place birthday candles on play-dough cakes, copying the pattern of spots.

Knowledge and understanding of the world

★ Have a colour hunt: name a colour and ask each child to search for an item of that colour in your setting.

★ Draw around a shadow outside on a sunny morning. Check it at intervals throughout the session and notice how it moves as the sun's position changes.

Physical development

★ Let the children assist you as you cut up fruit and vegetables and make a salad in the shape of a rainbow.

★ Thread wholewheat pasta onto string, and paint these 'beads' with PVA glue to make jewellery with an amber sheen.

Creative development

★ Collect an assortment of coloured footwear and create a shoe shop in your role-play area. Encourage the children to 'buy' their favourite-coloured pair of shoes.

★ Invite the children to sprinkle hundreds and thousands over buttered bread to make rainbow bread.

★ Make blobs of paint in different shades of blue onto plain wallpaper lying flat. Hang the paper up by the short edge to watch the drips run. Mount horizontally to represent the sea.

Early years wishing well: Colours and shapes

If peas were red

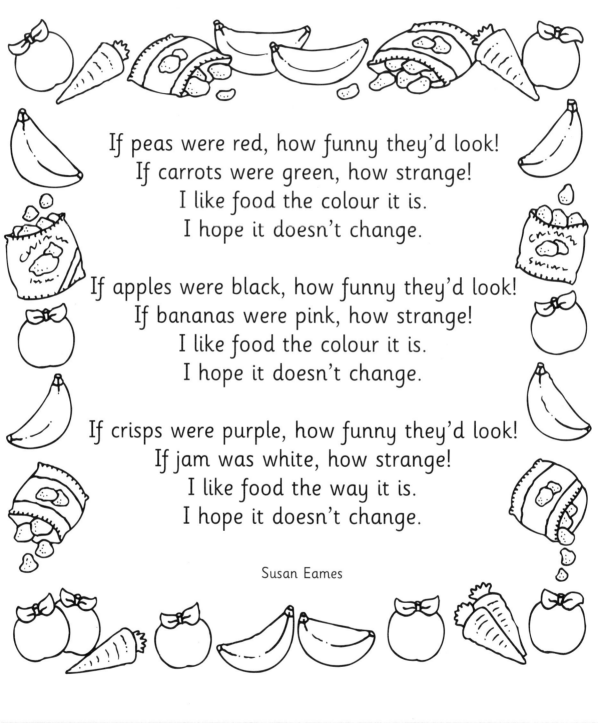

If peas were red, how funny they'd look!
If carrots were green, how strange!
I like food the colour it is.
I hope it doesn't change.

If apples were black, how funny they'd look!
If bananas were pink, how strange!
I like food the colour it is.
I hope it doesn't change.

If crisps were purple, how funny they'd look!
If jam was white, how strange!
I like food the way it is.
I hope it doesn't change.

Susan Eames

If peas were red

Personal, social and emotional development

★ Plan a simple menu with the children to cook and serve to guests, such as picnic food for little brothers and sisters, or soup, bread rolls and butter for elderly people in a local nursing home.

★ Bring in photographs and samples of unusual food from different cultures and diets for the children to discuss and try.

Communication, language and literacy

★ Challenge the children to say this tongue-twister: 'Purple butter, orange honey, blue jam, black bread. Spread it thick, say it quick!'.

★ Ask the children to make menus for the 'Crazy café' (see 'Creative development'), using the menu template on the photocopiable sheet on page 80. Encourage them to invent strange food such as purple banana soup or red pea fairy cakes.

Mathematical development

★ Dye some rice with bright food colouring and use it to measure the volume of various containers. Count how many large tablespoons of rice it takes to fill the largest container and encourage the children to guess how many tablespoons it will take to fill the others.

★ Ask the children to make you a pretend meal using Plasticine. Make requests such as, 'I'd like seven green peas, two brown sausages and three yellow potatoes'.

Knowledge and understanding of the world

★ Take the lenses out of toy sun-glasses and replace them with coloured Cellophane. Let the children wear the glasses and discuss whether they think food looks more or less appealing in a different colour.

★ Encourage the children to sort a collection of fruit and vegetables into 'sinkers' and 'floaters'. Use dyed water and watch the 'sinkers' change colour when viewed through the water.

★ Place food in sealed plastic bags and watch how the colour changes as it starts to decay: potatoes go green, cut apples go brown and bread goes green with mould. Dispose of the items carefully afterwards.

Physical development

★ Invite the children to help you make mashed potatoes, showing them how to use equipment safely and making sure they all have a go at mashing.

Creative development

★ Make salt-dough food with the children and paint it in strange colours. Use in the home corner as props for a 'Crazy café'.

★ Show the children still-life pictures of fruit such as those in *A Child's Book of Art* by Lucy Micklethwait (Dorling Kindersley), emphasizing how real they look. Make a simple display of fruit for the children to draw using pastels in the 'wrong' colours.

Creature colours

(Action rhyme)

Elephant, elephant,
great and grey,
lumbering along
with a slow, heavy sway.

*(make a rounded elephant
shape and lumber to the
rhythm)*

Ladybird, ladybird,
tickly and tiny,
red and black pattern
on a shell so shiny.

*(hold ladybird on open
hand and count spots
with index finger of other
hand)*

Tall giraffe, tall giraffe,
gazing quietly down,
what a long neck
all yellow and brown.

*(hold up arm to make
giraffe's neck, tilting hand
down to make giraffe's
head; run index finger of
other hand down the
giraffe's neck in time to the
line 'what a long neck')*

*(make butterfly with two hands
fluttering, thumbs linked, for first two
lines; then for last two lines separate
hands in surprise to show dramatic
astonishment)*

Butterfly, butterfly,
landing on the wall,
what a lot of colours...
you're the brightest one of all!

Use this model to write further verses to fit other creatures and their colours.

Tony Mitton

Creature colours

Personal, social and emotional development

★ Read some poems about wildlife to the children and talk about caring for living things.
★ Using the photocopiable sheet on page 81, make sets of beetle body parts on card. Invite the children to play 'Beetle' in small groups by rolling a dice and following the numbered key to make a whole beetle.

Communication, language and literacy

★ Display information books on animals and ask the children to use them to find pictures of animals of particular colours.
★ Let the children listen to *Elmer* by David McKee (available on tape as a *Tellastory* pack from Random House).
★ Make initial-sound mobiles. Cut out large animal shapes from pieces of card and ask the children to draw or stick pictures of items that have the same initial sound onto them.

Mathematical development

★ Using a toy zoo, develop positional language by placing zoo animals 'in the pond', 'on the wall' or 'under a tree'.
★ Make a set of 'feely' numerals based on animal textures.
★ Make a set of ladybirds, by copying the photocopiable sheet on page 81 onto red card, and number them 1 to 10. Invite the children to add black play-dough spots to match the ladybird's number.

Knowledge and understanding of the world

★ Take the children on a ladybird hunt, observing variations on colour and number of spots. Talk about the ladybird's wings being protected by the spotted wing case.
★ Talk about the rhyme and ask the children if they know what the animals look like.

Physical development

★ Read the poem 'Jump or Jiggle' by Evelyn Beyer from *Poems for the Very Young* edited by Michael Rosen (Kingfisher Books) and encourage the children to move like the animals mentioned.
★ Cut out butterfly shapes from kitchen roll. Invite the children to fold them in half and drip on diluted food colouring using a dropper. Leave the folded paper to dry, then open it to reveal patterns.

Creative development

★ Paint paper plates red or yellow, cut them in half and paint black spots on to make two ladybird wing cases with black bin-bag wings underneath. Paint other paper plates black to make the body and attach the wings and wing cases using split-pin fasteners so that they can be folded in and out. Add a round piece of black card for the head and black pipe-cleaners for the legs.
★ Make butterfly sandwiches. Let the children decorate buttered bread triangles with cheese, fruit and vegetable pieces.

Favourite colours

Which is your favourite colour
Red, yellow or blue?
Or do you like orange or purple?
Some people don't and some people do.

We each have a favourite colour.
Ask you friends and see what they say.
You might be surprised by the answers.
Perhaps green is their favourite today.

If I had to choose a colour
I'd pick a lovely sky-blue
With a rainbow shining across it
Showing colours of every hue.

Barbara Garrad

Early years wishing well: Colours and shapes

Favourite colours

Personal, social and emotional development

★ Arrange for the children to wear their favourite colours for the session. Ask them to do this again a few weeks later and discuss whether anyone's choice has changed. Talk about colours reflecting how we feel.

★ Encourage everyone to bring in something in a favourite colour to share at circle time.

★ Ask the children to use their favourite colours to make cards for a friend or family member.

Communication, language and literacy

★ Invite the children to make handprints in their favourite colour on card. When they are dry, cut them out and use them as name cards.

★ Ask the children to look out for signs and labels on billboards, packaging, in magazines and so on, written in their favourite colour.

★ Tape three crayons together and use them to make instant rainbow writing patterns.

Mathematical development.

★ Can the children spin a number wheel and either collect or put back that number of coloured cubes or counters, each child collecting a different colour? The aim is to make a collection of ten.

★ Invite each child to stick a coloured gummed square in their favourite colour onto squared paper. Group different colours in columns to make a graph showing the most popular colour and so on.

Knowledge and understanding of the world

★ Place white carnations in water dyed with food colouring. Invite the children to watch as they gradually change colour.

★ Take the children for a nature walk and, back at your setting, make a list of all the different colours that they observed. Which one do they like best?

★ Make coloured viewers by sandwiching coloured Cellophane between two paper plates with the middle discs removed. Which colour do the children most like to view things in?

Physical development

★ Sing 'If You're Happy and You Know It' changing the words to 'If your favourite colour's (red), clap your hands'.

★ Gather together coloured clothing with zips and buttons. Ask the children to volunteer to put on an item of clothing in a favourite colour and demonstrate for the group how to do it up.

Creative development

★ Sort materials such as sweet-wrappers, tissue paper and so on into separate tubs, one for each colour of the rainbow.

★ Make 'watery wonders' to shake, the children putting favourite colours of dyed water, glitter, sequins and foil confetti inside screw-top plastic bottles.

★ Encourage the children to paint a picture of something in their favourite colour, such as green leaves or a red post-box.

Hair colours

Fair hair, red hair,
Brown hair, black hair,
What does it matter
About the rest.
I love my hair,
Black and curly,
Plaited in patterns,
Mine's the best.
Tied in bunches
With ribbons of red,
Or threaded with beads
Around my head.

Jan Pollard

Early years wishing well: Colours and shapes

Hair colours

Personal, social and emotional development

★ Using pictures from magazines and books, make a montage of hair-styles from around the world. Display them with clips, brushes, beads and other hair products.

★ Talk about how hair changes at different stages of life, from babies through to old age. Make a 'hair time line' using magazine photographs.

Communication, language and literacy

★ Ask the children to think of words that rhyme with hair and scribe them on a cut-out head shape.

★ Place hair-related products in a bag. Make a set of cards showing shadow drawings of the items. Using touch only, ask a child to describe an item in detail, so that the other children can select the corresponding card.

Mathematical development

★ Draw patterns of threaded coloured beads on cut-out card heads and place these on a table with lengths of string and a selection of coloured beads. Can the children copy the patterns by threading the beads themselves?

★ Invite the children to sort hair ribbons by colour, length and width.

★ Make a market stall in the role-play area selling hair-related products. Encourage the children to price the products and play at buying and selling them.

Knowledge and understanding of the world

★ Looking at pets such as rabbits, mice and dogs, observe animal hair and fur. (**NB** Check for any allergies and ensure hands are washed thoroughly afterwards.)

★ Draw the outline of a man's face on card and seal this in a clear box or wallet with iron filings. Invite the children to move the filings around using a magnet, giving the man hair and a beard.

★ Add shampoo to water and provide whisks to make bubbles.

Physical development

★ Invite the children to make play-dough hair using a garlic press. Use it to decorate faces cut from magazines, or children's own pictures of themselves.

★ Talk about keeping hair clean and healthy. Encourage children to wash, dry and brush dolls' hair.

★ Provide ribbons and hair accessories so that children can practise braiding and tying hair.

Creative development

★ Provide mirrors, wigs, hair accessories, and stick-on moustaches and beards for the children to invent a new look!

★ Make a group wall-hanging using ribbons and beads.

★ Ask the children to paint themselves or their friends with weird and wonderful new hair-styles!

17

The wonderful coat of colours

Many, many years ago there was a boy called Joseph who had *eleven* brothers, and ten were older than he was! Their father was a rich farmer called Jacob, and Joseph was his favourite son.

When Joseph's older brothers saw their father making a fuss of Joseph, or giving him presents, they were very jealous.

'He never makes such a fuss of any of us!' they grumbled.

They felt so badly about Joseph that they could hardly talk to him.

When Joseph was seventeen, his father bought him a wonderful birthday present: it was a fantastic coat made from cloth that had every colour of the rainbow woven into it. Reds, blues, greens, yellows, pinks and purples. Shiny gold and silver. It was magnificent! As Joseph turned, the coat shone and sparkled in the sun. He felt really good in it – just like a prince. When Joseph's brothers saw that coat, you can imagine just how they felt. They were so cross! 'Dad never gave any of us such a good present!' they complained.

One day, when Joseph's brothers were looking after the sheep up in the hills, Jacob sent Joseph to find them, to make sure they were all right. Joseph set out on the long journey, wearing his wonderful coat.

While he was still quite far away, his brothers saw the colours of his coat shining in the sun: reds, blues, greens, yellows, pinks and purples.

Shiny gold and silver. They knew it was Joseph's.

'Now's our chance,' they said. 'We can get rid of Joseph for good!'

'No,' said the eldest brother. 'We must not hurt him. We'll just throw him into an empty well and leave him there. Someone will find him.'

So that's what they did. When Joseph arrived, the unkind brothers tore off his magnificent, colourful coat and threw Joseph roughly down a well.

Just then some traders rode by with their camels. This gave the brothers an idea. They *sold* Joseph to the traders for twenty silver coins!

Suddenly Joseph found himself tied to a camel and on his way to Egypt!

His brothers took Joseph's wonderful coat and covered it with goat's blood. Then they took it back to Jacob. Poor Jacob was sure that a lion had killed Joseph and that he would never see him again.

But Joseph was to have many strange adventures in Egypt and he became a very important person. He had *many* wonderful clothes to wear every day - although none of them were quite as amazing as that coat his father had given him.

And he did see his father and his brothers again – but that's another story.

Retold by Jackie Andrews
(Taken from Genesis, chapter 37)

Early years wishing well: Colours and shapes

Colours

Stories

The wonderful coat of colours

Personal, social and emotional development

★ Talk about times when life does not seem fair. Was it fair to give nice presents to only one son?

★ Encourage the children to think of ways to be considerate to others. Take photographs to make a display, and add captions such as, 'Ben and Kathryn are sharing toys' and 'Tom is tidying up'.

Communication, language and literacy

★ Make parcel-shaped booklets with ribbon ties. Ask the children to draw and write about a favourite present inside.

★ Ask the children to draw simple versions of illuminated letters, like those often found in Bibles, on strips of card. They can then write the other letters of their name neatly to make name cards.

★ Read the rest of the story of Joseph to the children. *The Children's Illustrated Bible* edited by Selina Hastings (Dorling Kindersley) has a version of the story, with factual information and pictures of Egypt.

Mathematical development

★ Talk about the traders in the story and set up a spice shop in the role-play area where the children can measure powdered spices into packets, count whole ones and use scales to balance the spices with pieces of 'silver' (pebbles sprayed silver). Exchange the 'silver' for the spices.

★ Give the children foreign currency to examine and compare with our own.

★ Ask the children to hang 'age' birthday cards on a number line in order.

Knowledge and understanding of the world

★ Invite the children to dye white fabric with natural dyes from plants. Try pomegranate rinds, pine cones, beetroot, spinach and onion skins. Provide protective gloves and aprons.

★ Look at pictures of Egypt. Compare the natural features and style of buildings with those in the children's locality.

★ Ask the children to polish brass and copper items until they shine, wearing gloves to avoid allergic reactions.

★ Display a collection of coats made from different materials.

Physical development

★ Wrap up boxes and pieces of material to make a pile of presents. Help the children to cut the paper, use sticky tape and tie ribbons around the parcels.

★ Encourage the children to pretend to ride camels and climb in and out of the well.

Creative development

★ Invite the children to cut out camel or sheep shapes from card, decorate them with wool and add a pair of pegs for legs.

★ Create a collage of Joseph's coat using paper, fabric and glitter to make stripes.

Serena's favourite colour

'Mrs Stephens taught us a song about colours!' Serena said to her mother as they left nursery school that day. 'And tomorrow we've got to wear our favourite colour and Mrs Stephens wants to take a photo of us!'

'That's great,' said her mum. 'What colour would you like to wear?'

Serena thought and thought, but she couldn't choose.

At home, Serena looked around her bedroom. When she saw her cuddly brown teddy, Serena thought brown was her favourite colour. But then she saw her silver shoes and thought silver was the colour she liked best.

In the bathroom, Serena really liked the soft green of the towels. But then she looked at her mum's fluffy purple slippers with the pink butterflies on them, and she thought that purple and pink were prettier.

Downstairs, Serena looked at her dad's blue track suit and thought that maybe she liked blue best...but when she spotted her brother's goldfish swimming round their tank, she decided bright orange was even nicer.

Serena went outside into the garden. As she fed her lop-eared rabbit and stroked his soft, black fur, she thought she really liked black. But then she saw the white daisies with their yellow centres, and yellow and white became her favourites.

Serena simply couldn't decide which of all these beautiful colours she liked best.

Next morning, she told her mum just how difficult it was to choose one colour.

'But I really want to be in the photograph!' she said.

'Don't worry, Serena,' said her mum. 'I've got an idea...'

Mrs Stephens' nursery class lit up with colours as the children all arrived that morning and took their places on the mat. Serena kept her blue raincoat on as one by one the children told the class their favourite colours.

Then it was Serena's turn. She stood up and took off her coat.

'Oh, Serena's got a *red* skirt!' said one of the children. 'Red's her favourite colour – just like mine!'

'But she's got a *green* belt!' said another.

'And a *yellow* T-shirt!'

'She's got a *pink* necklace!'

'Look at her *silver* shoes – and she's got one *blue* sock and one *orange* one!'

'And her ribbon's *purple*!'

'So which colour did you choose, Serena?' Mrs Stephens asked.

'*All* of them!' said Serena.

Everyone laughed and clapped.

Mrs Stephens picked up her camera.

'Come and sit in the middle, Serena. You look as pretty as a rainbow in all your favourite colours.'

Geraldine Taylor

Early years wishing well: Colours and shapes

Serena's favourite colour

Personal, social and emotional development

★ Plan a 'favourite clothes day' with the children and invite them to take photographs. Take some yourself to display afterwards.

★ Give six pairs of socks to a group of six children. Ask each child to put on two different socks. Play some music and see if the children can sit in a circle and match pairs of socks together before the music stops.

Communication, language and literacy

★ Cut pictures from catalogues of the places that Serena visited. Stick the four locations randomly onto paper and laminate. Do this enough times for each child to have their own version. Give each child a non-permanent marker and ask them to follow the sequence of rooms by marking a line on their paper.

★ Develop vocabulary by investigating items which are cuddly, fluffy or soft.

★ Ask the children to decorate clothes shapes with writing patterns.

Mathematical development

★ Make a copy for each child of the photocopiable sheet on page 82. Roll a dice and follow the key to colour in the clothing.

★ Ask everyone to bring in a piece of clothing in their favourite colour. Use for sorting and counting activities.

★ Carry out a simple survey. Encourage the children to make a list of colours that they can ask each other to choose from, then count up the votes to identify the most popular colour for clothing in the group.

Knowledge and understanding of the world

★ Talk about what the children have in their bedrooms and bathrooms. Compare this with pictures in information books of these rooms in the past.

★ Invite the children to bring in a white T-shirt to dye in a favourite colour, using cold water dyes. Ensure the area and the children are well protected.

Physical development

★ Pretend to get dressed using words such as, 'Now we put on our bright red socks' to the tune of 'Here We Go Round the Mulberry Bush'.

★ Ask some children to 'leap like rabbits and swim like fish' while others provide the rhythm with percussion instruments.

Creative development

★ Look at the colours and textures of daisies. Encourage the children to use paint to make daisies with a circle of white handprints for the petals and yellow finger dots for the centres.

★ Learn a song about colours, for example, 'I Know a Man Called Mr Red' from *This Little Puffin…* compiled by Elizabeth Matterson (Puffin Books).

Early years wishing well: Colours and shapes

The perfect picture

Once upon a time, there was a princess who loved painting. But she could never find the right colours for her pictures. Her blues looked like dishwater; her reds like mud; her yellows like dust; and her greens like cabbage.

'I shall never paint a perfect picture,' she sighed, 'until I find a blue as bright as the sea, a red as deep as a rose, a yellow as golden as the sun and a green as cool as the grass.'

Now the time came for the princess to find a husband, so she said, 'I will marry the man who can bring me a blue that is as bright as the sea.'

One day a handsome prince came riding by and said, 'Princess, I will find you a blue as bright as the sea.'

He rode till he came to the edge of the bright blue sea. The prince took a single drop in a shell and rode back to the princess.

'Oh, thank you,' she said. 'It's perfect.'

'Princess, will you marry me?' asked the prince.

'No,' said the princess, 'not unless you can bring me a red as deep as a rose.'

So the prince rode till he came to a beautiful garden, where he found a rose of the deepest, deepest red. Taking a single bloom, he rode back to the princess.

'Oh, thank you,' she said. 'It's perfect.'

'Princess, now will you marry me?' asked the prince.

'No Prince, I cannot marry you until you find me a yellow that is as golden as the sun.'

So the prince rode till he reached a burning hot desert. There he caught a ray of sun in a handful of sparkling, golden sand, and rode back to the princess.

'Oh, thank you,' she said. 'It's perfect.'

'Princess, now will you marry me?' he asked.

'No Prince, I cannot marry you until you find me a green that is as cool as grass.'

So the prince rode to the top of a high mountain where he found grass of the coolest, freshest green. Taking a single blade, he rode back to the princess.

'Oh, thank you,' she said. 'Now I can paint a perfect picture.'

'Princess, *now* will you marry me?' asked the Prince.

'Oh no, Prince,' she replied. 'I'm much too busy painting.'

So the prince married a princess who liked cookery instead, and they lived happily ever after.

Julia Moffatt

Early years wishing well: Colours and shapes

The perfect picture

Personal, social and emotional development

★ Create a beautiful group painting, containing all the colours mentioned in the story.

★ Share ideas on how the story could end for the princess. Was it right for her not to keep her promise?

★ Ask each family to contribute a favourite simple recipe and compile a cookery book that is fit for a prince!

Communication, language and literacy

★ Read stories about princesses, both traditional, such as 'The Princess and the Pea', and modern, such as The Little Princess series by Tony Ross (Andersen Press). Do they all live happily ever after?

★ Encourage the children to write their name with a glue pen and sprinkle on coloured sand and glitter.

★ The princess wanted a blue 'as bright as the sea'. Using the phrases in the story, make a book for each colour illustrated with children's drawings.

Mathematical development

★ With paint, colour water blue and ask the children to count how many drops of blue water will fill a selection of small shells.

★ Paint repeating patterns in the four colours of the story.

★ Test how many handfuls of sand it takes to fill a margarine tub, a bucket and so on.

Knowledge and understanding of the world

★ Select pictures and paintings of royalty long ago. Ask the children to look at the people and describe their clothes.

★ Invite the children to decorate a yoghurt pot with collage materials to look like a prince's face and body. Help them to fill it with compost and scatter grass seed on top to grow into hair.

★ Have a mini topic on roses, displaying paintings, plants, dried petals, scented and flavoured products.

★ Encourage each child to pretend to be the prince and go on a walk near your setting to observe examples of 'perfect' flowers, leaves, plants, trees and clouds.

Physical development

★ With coconut shells to direct the rhythm, encourage the children to pretend to ride horses, galloping, trotting, and changing speed and direction.

★ Choose a favourite recipe to cook together for an imaginary prince.

Creative development

★ Mix a small amount of thick paste with dyed blue water and place it in a zip-lock plastic bag. Add shells, green Cellophane and fish cut from plastic or Cellophane to make a sea world.

★ Using compost, gravel, grass seed and tiny plants, make miniature gardens on a foil plate.

The special day

For her sister Meena's wedding, Nazmeen was to wear the most beautiful shalwar kameez in the whole world. It was emerald green, all silky and shiny with glittering glass beads sewn in a swirly pattern.

Mum helped Nazmeen to dress, then said, 'It is early. You must sit still, Nazmeen, while I help Meena. Stay on the sofa and look at some books.'

Nazmeen, who felt like a beautiful princess, nodded her head.

'Remember!' said Mum. 'Don't move!' Then she swept out of the room, closed the door and went upstairs.

Just then, Nazmeen heard a voice calling through the fence in the back garden. 'Nazmeen! Nazmeen!'

Nazmeen opened the back door and peered out.

'Nazmeen! Nazmeen! Come out and play!'

It was her friend, Nicole.

'I can't come out, Nicole!' Nazmeen shouted. 'I'm dressed for the wedding.'

'Oh, Nazmeen, show me your wedding clothes!' called Nicole.

Nazmeen answered, 'I can't, Nicole!'

Nicole called again. 'Nazmeen, just let me see you! *Please!*'

Nazmeen thought, *It would only take a minute, wouldn't it?* She really wanted Nicole to see her looking like a princess. Very slowly, she pushed open the back door, stepped down into the garden and ran.

But as she ran, oh dear! Nazmeen tripped on the cobbles of the patio. Over she went, into a large, muddy puddle.

The beautiful, emerald-green silk shalwar kameez was covered with muddy water!

Nicole's eyes opened wide through the gap in the fence. 'Oh, Nazmeen, you're all dirty!'

Nazmeen burst into tears. What would happen now?

Upstairs in the bedroom, Mum heard Nazmeen cry. She looked out of the window, and then she ran downstairs, scooped Nazmeen up and rushed back into the house with her.

'Quick! Quick!' she shouted as she bustled Nazmeen into the bathroom. She sponged the muddy water from the beautiful emerald-green silk shalwar kameez before it had a chance to soak in, then she put it on the radiator to dry. Downstairs came Meena in her wonderful bride's sari of red and gold.

'We are still too early,' said Mum. 'Meena – you had better sit on the sofa to wait. No going into the garden to show Nicole your wedding clothes!'

When at last the beautiful emerald-green silk shalwar kameez had dried, everyone agreed that Nazmeen still looked like a princess. Then they all had a very special hug, because it was such a very special day.

Irene Yates

Early years wishing well: Colours and shapes

Colours Stories

The special day

Personal, social and emotional development

★ Role-play being Nazmeen getting ready for the wedding and falling over. Ask the children to suggest different ways her Mum might have reacted.

★ Invite representatives of the major religions to your setting, or arrange a visit to their places of worship, to look at artefacts and talk about marriage ceremonies.

Communication, language and literacy

★ Encourage the children to role-play being at a celebratory meal. Invite them to write their names on their own place cards and to decorate them.

★ Introduce vocabulary associated with special celebrations, clothes and people, using photographs as a prompt.

★ Make copies of the photocopiable sheet on page 83 and ask the children to cut the pictures out and sequence Nazmeen's story to make a zigzag book.

Mathematical development

★ Use a variety of timers to let the children test the length of time that they can sit still.

★ Investigate how long a minute is and what tasks the children can complete in that time, such as threading beads or building a tower of bricks.

★ Create a 'wedding cake' by stacking boxes in size order.

Knowledge and understanding of the world

★ Make a collection of shining, glittering objects and hang them up near a window to catch the light.

★ Ask the children to wash clothes and compare how long they take to dry scrunched up, flat, on a radiator and outside.

Physical development

★ Dance, walk and march to music traditionally played at weddings, such as *Toccata* (JS Bach).

★ Draw a path for the children to run, skip, hop and jump along. Mark areas that are puddles and tell the children that they must not step on them.

★ Plan and hold a role-play wedding with invitations, a ceremony and a reception.

Creative development

★ Design and make jewellery using pasta, beads, rolled paper, braid and sequins.

★ Make a wedding 'misfit book' in three parts: heads, bodies and feet. Help the children to cut pictures from magazines and divide them into three sections to make interchangeable brides, grooms, attendants and guests.

★ Encourage the children to paint a picture of Nazmeen in her emerald-green shalwar kameez (long tunic with matching under-trousers) and to decorate it with beads, sweet-wrappers, braiding, sequins and so on.

Early years wishing well: Colours and shapes

Jack and the balloon picture

Jack had decided to paint a balloon picture.

First, he drew ten big balloons on his sheet of paper. Some were round and some were sausage-shaped. There were long, thin ones and short, fat ones.

He dipped his brush in the red paint and made a beautiful, shiny, red balloon. Red was his favourite colour.

He cleaned his brush carefully in the water jar, then used the blue paint. After that, he did the same with the yellow. Each time Jack wiped his brush on the edge of the pot so that the paint didn't dribble down and spoil his picture.

Jack now had three balloons in his picture: red, blue and yellow. But there was still a number of balloons left... Seven! He would have to mix some of the colours together if they were all going to be different.

So Jack took a clean brush and poured some red and yellow paint into a small dish. He mixed them with his brush and made...orange! Jack painted an orange sausage balloon.

Next he mixed up some blue and red paint and made...purple! Jack painted a big, fat, purple balloon.

Then he mixed blue and yellow paint and made...green! Jack painted a long, thin, green balloon.

Jack thought he'd try mixing red and green together. It made a rich brown. So Jack painted a large, round, brown balloon.

How many balloons were left? Jack counted them. Three.

Jack washed his brush carefully again and dipped it into the white paint. He painted a fat, white balloon. Then he made a long, black balloon with the black paint. But there was still one balloon left. Jack thought hard. He would just have to mix all the colours together!

And that's just what he did. They made a very funny, purply-brown colour for the last balloon, but the picture was really colourful, and Jack's teacher liked it so much she put it up on the wall.

Val Jeans-Jakobsson

Early years wishing well: Colours and shapes

Jack and the balloon picture

Personal, social and emotional development

★ Encourage the children to reflect on birthdays, fairs or other special occasions at which they may have seen balloons.
★ Talk about handling balloons safely and disposing of them properly.

Communication, language and literacy

★ Make a display of inflated and deflated balloons. Use them to introduce vocabulary relating to balloons, looking at surface texture, shape, size and so on.
★ Invite the children to write their names onto balloons. Fasten each balloon onto a chair while the children are out. Can they find their chair when they come back in?
★ Fill balloons with air, water, flour and wet sand and seal them securely. Pass the balloons around a circle, discussing how they feel.

Mathematical development

★ Copy the balloon game from the photocopiable sheet on page 84. Play *Lotto* using shapes or colours.
★ Roll a dice marked with the numerals 0, 1 and 2 on three sides and with dots on the other three. Using the photocopiable sheet on page 84, the children should colour the corresponding number of balloons, throwing the dice until they reach a total of exactly eight.
★ Ask the children to sponge-print ten balloons and number them when they are dry.

Knowledge and understanding of the world

★ Compare helium and air-filled balloons and look at photographs of hot-air balloons.
★ Blow up two identical balloons and observe how they move when you throw them into the air. Repeat with one balloon containing more air than the other.
★ Tie lengths of string to balloons and take them outside on a windy day to watch how they move. Try again on a still day and compare the effect.

Physical development

★ Time how long a group of children can keep a balloon in the air.
★ Pretend to be limp balloons without air in them, expanding as they are blown up and then floating. Finish the mime by popping!
★ Make shakers by dropping different pulses and rice into balloons before inflating them with a pump.

Creative development

★ Encourage the children to mix colours when painting balloon pictures. Compare the colours made, are they all the same?
★ Invite the children to create patterns by printing with partly inflated balloons.
★ Encourage the children to use black felt-tipped pens to draw simple pictures on non-inflated balloons. Let them observe how their pictures get bigger when the balloons are blown up.

The farm

Dad has brought some boxes from work so we can make a model farm together. One box is very big but flat, like a tray. Dad says it is just right for the farmyard because the sides can be the fences around the farm.

First, we have to paint all the sides brown so that they look like a wooden fence. I fetch my paints and put on my apron while Mum quickly covers the table with newspaper so we don't make a mess.

Dad says he never makes a mess so *he* doesn't need an apron.

We paint all the sides of the box brown. Then we paint inside the box brown, too. Dad gets a blob of brown paint on his nose.

We leave the fence to dry and start to make the farmhouse. Dad picks up a small box and cuts some holes out of the front for windows. Then he makes a door. He tells me to paint the farmhouse any colour that I want, so I paint the roof red, the walls white and the door purple.

Dad leans over to paint a knocker on the door and his tie dangles in the black paint. But he doesn't notice.

The fence is dry now, so we can finish painting the farm. Dad draws a squiggly path and a pond on the bottom of the box. We paint the pond blue but we don't know what colour to paint the path. I look at all the colours we've used: red, white, purple, brown, blue and black...and decide I want a yellow path. So we paint the path yellow and the grass green.

Dad gets a bit of green paint on his shirt, but he doesn't notice.

I go upstairs and fetch my farmer, tractor and farm animals. When I come back down the paint is dry so I can put them all into the model farm and play with them. It's the best farm in the world.

When Dad clears away the paints he splashes blue and yellow paint over his face but he doesn't notice. He tells Mum that she didn't have to worry: he hasn't made a mess.

Mum looks at me and winks.

Karen King

Early years wishing well: Colours and shapes

The farm

Personal, social and emotional development

★ Make a farm from a box for your small-world farm animals. Share ideas about what to paint on it, such as paddocks, a barn or a duck pond.

★ Dress up as a farmer and fill a sack with small-world farm animals. Sing 'Old MacDonald' while the children pass the sack around, taking out an item and singing a verse about it. Place them on the farm base.

Communication, language and literacy

★ Give the children copies of the photocopiable sheet on page 85 and ask them to use a pencil to follow the dotted lines leading the animals to their homes.

★ Collect pairs of identical boxes, such as cereal boxes. Cut the product name from one of the boxes in each pair, and ask the children to find the matching word on the second box.

★ Sing 'I Went to Visit a Farm One Day' from *This Little Puffin…* compiled by Elizabeth Matterson (Puffin Books) while passing around a bag containing farm-animal masks. Take turns to wear a mask and make the animal's sound.

Mathematical development

★ Make a flat tray from cardboard which will fit a set of different-sized small boxes placed side by side. Challenge the children to fit them in.

★ Take three different-sized boxes and ask the children which one will hold the most toy farm animals and which will hold the fewest.

Knowledge and understanding of the world

★ Give the children paint-covered fabrics to wash with and without detergents in warm and cold water. Compare the results.

★ Look at and discuss different ways that toy tractors can be powered or moved, such as pushing, pulling, clockwork or batteries.

★ Sing 'Little Boy Blue' and provide information books with pictures of farms from long ago and today for the children to compare.

Physical development

★ Teach the children how to wink, and discuss the difference between blinking and winking.

★ Photograph a series of simple arrangements of cardboard boxes. Give them to the children for them to try and copy.

★ Make an obstacle course for the children to move around on tractors. Provide various soft farm animals along the way for the children to collect.

Creative development

★ Using toy tractors, invite the children to make tyre prints with paint.

★ Make farm animals from recyclable materials.

★ Look at farm paintings by John Constable and Pieter Bruegel and compare the colours and content with the children's paintings.

Early years wishing well: Colours and shapes

Black and blue!

(Tune: 'Hot Cross Buns')

1. Black means rain, gales and hail, An-gry clouds will soak the crowds, yes black means rain.

2. Brighter now,
Lighter now,
Seven colours make a rainbow
Brighter now.

3. Blue means sun,
Lots of fun,
Sun shines bright and all is right
Yes blue means sun.

Peter Morrell

Early years wishing well: Colours and shapes

Black and blue!

Personal, social and emotional development

★ Pass around a rain stick and share ideas about what to do on a rainy day.
★ Talk about sun safety and remind the children never to look directly at the sun.
★ Copy the weather chart from the photocopiable sheet on page 86. Decide as a group what the weather is like that day and choose different children to fill the chart in, using the key as reference.

Communication, language and literacy

★ Encourage the children to use chalk to write their names on the ground. Watch what happens when it rains.
★ Share some traditional sayings about the sky and weather, for example: 'A sunshiny shower won't last half an hour' and 'Red sky at night, shepherd's delight'.

Mathematical development

★ Using your weather chart, keep a count of how many days you have of each type of weather over a two-week period or longer. Invite the children to count them and work out which type of weather you have had the most of.
★ Collect a variety of coloured wellington boots and invite the children to match them to coloured card 'puddles'. Count how many pairs there are of each colour and how many in total.

Knowledge and understanding of the world

★ Cut out coat shapes from different materials. Ask the children to spray them with water. Which coat stops the 'crowds from being soaked'?
★ Stand a clear plastic bottle of water on white paper in sunlight. Challenge the children to make rainbows by changing the bottle's position.
★ Pour water on concrete on a sunny day and help the children to chalk around the shape it makes. Check it regularly and repeat the chalking, noticing how the shape and size of the puddle changes.

Physical development

★ Encourage the children to blow bubbles and look for the rainbow colours.
★ Mime a wet-day walk: putting on wellington boots, putting up umbrellas, splashing in puddles and so on.

Creative development

★ Make wet weather pictures by sprinkling powder paint onto wet paper. Spray with water and hold up to make a rainy effect.
★ Make a group mobile for the song. Organize the children into separate groups to make: a bright collage sun, a painted rainbow and raindrops created by adding drops of PVA glue to lengths of string.
★ Mix shades of blue and grey paints for the children to create rainy-day pictures with.

Early years wishing well: Colours and shapes

Camouflage, camouflage

2. Can you see an insect when it's like a stick? NO!
Can you see a moth that plays the tree bark trick? NO!
Can you spot a leopard when it's got the chicken pox? NO! So,
How are we supposed to know it's there?
CHORUS

Peter Morrell

Early years wishing well: Colours and shapes

Camouflage, camouflage

Personal, social and emotional development

★ Provide camouflage clothes and explain to the children that they are bird-watchers who are trying to remain hidden. Invite them to throw a dice in turn until it lands on six. The person who has thrown the six tries to put on all the clothes before the next six is thrown.

★ Cut pictures from wildlife magazines showing animal prints. Enlarge them on the photocopier and cut them in half. Fasten the halves onto pairs of children and let the rest of the group match the pairs.

Communication, language and literacy

★ Mount pictures of animals on animal-print paper and write their names, highlighting the initial letter. Display them along an alphabet frieze by the correct letter.

★ Select magazine pages that have different styles of print and glue them onto card. Using the template on the photocopiable sheet on page 87 as a guide, cut identical moth shapes out of the pages. Muddle the pages up and ask the children to match the cut-out moth shapes with the pages they come from.

Mathematical development

★ Make a copy of the photocopiable sheet on page 87, cut out the template for each child and let them decorate their moths. Help each child to add different numbers of spots from 1 to 10 and use for the following activities.

★ Match moths to number cards.
★ Place moths in number order along a branch.
★ Count the dots to find two moths that equal a given number when added together.

Knowledge and understanding of the world

★ Compare the colours used in camouflage clothing (browns, greens) with those used for visibility, such as fluorescent safety jackets.

★ Display pictures and books showing camouflaged stick insects (or show the children a real one if possible). Play a game to see who can spot the animals first, and talk about the way they blend into their surroundings.

Physical development

★ Play 'Hide-and-seek' in dull clothes, then in bright clothes.

★ Whisk soap flakes and water until stiff. Use the mixture to make a polar landscape, hiding toy polar bears for the children to find.

Creative development

★ Invite the children to draw around the moth template (photocopiable sheet on page 87) onto brown wrapping paper decorated with bark rubbings and then to 'hide' their moths in a collage of natural materials.

★ Ask the children to make stick insects from rolled-up paper and art straws and paint them. Display them on a branch of the same colour.

Food colours

(Tune: 'Twinkle, Twinkle, Little Star')

1. What do we eat that's green, green, green? What do we eat that's green, green, green?

Run - ner beans are al - ways green, Run - ner beans are al - ways green.

What do we eat that's green, green, green? Run - ner beans are al - ways green.

2. What do we eat that's red red red?
What do we eat that's red red red?
Strawberry jam is always red,
Strawberry jam is always red,
What do we eat that's red red red?
Strawberry jam is always red.

3. ...Wholemeal bread is always brown...

4. ...Natural yoghurt is always white...

5. ...Orange juice is always orange...

*Notes not in traditional tune

Ann Bryant

Early years wishing well: Colours and shapes

Food colours

Personal, social and emotional development

★ Give the children a bowl of multicoloured yoghurt-coated raisins to share out for a snack.

★ Invite the children to sit in a circle around a selection of foods and pass a basket around. Ask them to select a food in turn and, whilst putting it in the basket, to say 'I went shopping and I bought a (red tomato)', mentioning the food and its colour. Each child must repeat the previous phrase(s) before adding their own.

Communication, language and literacy

★ Encourage the children to make an edible name out of wholemeal bread using alphabet cutters.

★ Using pictures of food cut from magazines, ask the children to make a 'food colours' book with a different colour of food items on each page. Add a cover shaped like a mouth.

★ Set up a café in the home corner with the children taking turns to be customers, write down orders and make the food using play dough. Encourage the use of 'please' and 'thank you'.

Mathematical development

★ Chop a selection of green vegetables and fruit into large pieces and place them all on one plate. Challenge the children to make the whole items again, and then to count how many pieces each one was cut into.

★ Using a bucket balance, ask the children to identify the heaviest and the lightest of two green beans or oranges. Repeat with three of each item.

Knowledge and understanding of the world

★ Squeeze fresh oranges and invite the children to taste the juice. Encourage them to compare the packaging and taste of fresh, bottled, frozen, tinned and carton orange juice and to tell you which one they prefer and why.

★ Plant bean seeds and strawberry plants. Watch them grow and enjoy eating the results!

★ Cut up fruit and vegetables and compare the colour of their flesh to the one of their skin.

Physical development

★ Ask the children to spread different red jams onto wholemeal bread and to try and guess what fruits were used.

★ Invite each child to pour white Greek yoghurt into a bowl. Ask them to stir in strawberry jam and to watch how the colour changes.

Creative development

★ Invite the children to create edible art from fruit and vegetables. Look at pictures by Giuseppe Arcimboldo for inspiration.

★ Retell the story of 'Jack and the Beanstalk' (Traditional) to the children using finger puppets and real beans attached to a plant.

Little green man

Don't cross o-ver the road un-til the lit-tle green man ap-pears.

Don't cross o-ver the road un-til the lit-tle green man ap-pears. 1. If the

red man keeps you stand-ing there he's wait-ing 'til it's clear.

Don't cross o-ver the road un-til the lit-tle green man is here.

2. When the green man comes
He tells you by his beeping
That it's clear.

Clive Barnwell

Early years wishing well: Colours and shapes

Little green man

Personal, social and emotional development

★ Cut red and green men shapes from card, one green man to every four red men. Put them in a bag to pass around a circle while the children sing 'Skip, skip, skip round the circle (three times), If you get a green man', to the tune of 'Skip to My Lou'. The children take turns to pull a man from the bag and must skip once around the outside of the circle if it is green.

★ Ask the local road safety officer to visit your setting and talk to the children about crossing roads safely.

★ Play the game on the photocopiable sheet on page 88. Take three small-world play people in different colours, one dice marked with spots of these colours and one dice with three green and three red men. Ask three children to take turns rolling both dice. If the green man shows, move the piece matching the colour on the other dice one space. If the red man shows, the piece does not move. The winner is the first to get their piece to the play area.

Communication, language and literacy

★ Place a variety of items in a box. When those beginning with 'b' are taken out, make a 'beeping' sound.

★ Look at pictures in magazines and books of pedestrians in road scenes. Encourage the children to suggest what they might be saying to each other.

Mathematical development

★ Make a graph of the different ways that the children travel to your setting. Ask them if their journey incorporates crossing by a green man.

★ Ask the children to continue a repeating pattern made with red and green paint and people-sponges.

Knowledge and understanding of the world

★ Take a variety of noisy items and record their sounds onto a tape. Place the items that you have used in the centre of a circle while you play the tape. Challenge the children to listen and select the item that made each sound.

★ Make a pelican crossing and use it in role-play with sit 'n' ride vehicles.

Physical development

★ Go for a short walk and find a pelican crossing and a zebra crossing. Show the children how to cross them correctly.

★ Play 'Musical statues', walking around the room to music and standing still when the music stops.

Creative development

★ Use junk materials to make a 3D street with vehicles, paths and roads. Use small-world play people and cars, and cross the people safely over the road.

★ Give each child a percussion instrument and ask them to play it when you hold up a green man and stop when you hold up a red man.

Sky is so blue

(Tune: 'Lavender's blue')

1. Sky is so blue, did-dle did-dle, Grass is so green;

Each way I look, did-dle did-le, co-lours are seen.

2. Your car is black, diddle diddle,
My car is white;
Some cars are pale, diddle diddle,
Some cars are bright.

3. Some eyes are brown, diddle diddle,
Some eyes are blue;
Some eyes are green, diddle diddle,
Let's look at you!
(children turn to their neighbour to see their eye colour)

Johanne Levy

Early years wishing well: Colours and shapes

Sky is so blue

Personal, social and emotional development

★ Invite a guide dog and handler to your setting to talk to the children about how non-sighted people move around safely.

★ Cut pairs of eyes from magazines and mount them onto separate pieces of card. Ask the children to try to find matching pairs.

★ Play a game passing a stare or other eye expression around a circle.

Communication, language and literacy

★ Contact a local resource centre or library and obtain a familiar story, such as one of the *Spot* books by Eric Hill (Picture Puffin), that uses both Braille and printed words. Encourage the children to feel the Braille.

★ Make feely letters by sticking different textured materials to a selection of cardboard letters. Can the children recognize the letters by touch alone?

★ Fasten colour chips from paint charts onto toy cars and draw a car park onto card. Ask the children to park the cars, encouraging colour-based vocabulary such as, 'The blue car is parking next to the pink car'.

★ Play a game of 'Colour I spy'. Children can identify the object in question by asking questions such as, 'Is it lighter than this blue?'.

Mathematical development

★ Number a selection of toy cars. Ask the children to make a traffic jam with the numbers in sequence or drive the cars into numbered car park spaces.

★ Using a bucket balance, ask the children to find out how many fir cones, Lego bricks and so on, weigh the same as a toy car.

★ Make a graph of the children's eye colours.

Knowledge and understanding of the world

★ Make an obstacle course and encourage the children to drive a remote control car through it without it touching anything.

★ Sit each child on a large circular piece of paper and ask them to record which colours are seen in each direction. Let them draw themselves in the centre of the paper to complete their circular map.

Physical development

★ Ask the children to sprinkle grass seed onto trays of compost to grow small-world fields.

★ Invite the children to roll paper into tubes to use as viewers on a colour hunt.

Creative development

★ Make a role-play optician's with cardboard glasses for the children to decorate, eye-charts, mirrors and an appointment book.

★ Lie down and look at the sky on a cloudy day. (**NB** Warn the children about never looking directly at the sun.) Encourage the children to describe the colours they see. Follow up the activity by using pastels to create sky pictures.

White

(Tune: 'Here We Go Round the Mulberry Bush')

White is for su - gar, white for snow, and white's for pa - per so words will show.

White for the flour to make our bread, and white for clouds float - ing o - ver - head.

*Notes not in traditional tune

Sue Nicholls

Early years wishing well: Colours and shapes

White

Personal, social and emotional development

★ Mix together cornflour and just enough water to make a very thick mixture. Invite the children to try and pass it around a table from hand to hand without dropping any.

★ Gather together white items (clothing, sheets, cushions, pots, play food) to make a totally white imaginative play area.

★ Select photographs of homes, people, landscapes and transport here and in the Arctic. Encourage the children to compare their life with life in the Arctic using the photographs.

Communication, language and literacy

★ Make a collection of coloured packaging with white writing on it.

★ Using a white wax crayon on white paper, show the children how to make invisible writing. Add a colour wash to reveal it.

★ Read the story *Jolly Snow* by Jane Hissey (Red Fox). Talk about snow with the children. Have they ever seen thick snow? What games can people play in snow?

Mathematical development

★ Use white tubs, plastic spoons, paper cups, flour, salt and rice to investigate capacity.

★ Make 'snow' by mixing together shredded white tissue paper, soap flakes and warm water. Provide different-sized tubs and ask the children to make 'snow pies'. Use them for counting, size ordering and matching them to tubs.

★ Add polar bears to the 'snow' and develop positional language placing them under, on or between snow pies.

Knowledge and understanding of the world

★ Use white ingredients to make glovjamin, an Asian treat. Mix together one cup of self-raising flour, three cups of dried milk and fresh milk to make a firm dough. Roll into small balls, fry and when cool sprinkle with icing sugar.

★ Catch snow flakes on black fabric and observe them with magnifying glasses.

Physical development

★ Invite the children to build models with sugar cubes or ice blocks.

★ Help the children to fold and cut out snowflakes from white paper. Cover them in glue, and sprinkle on silver glitter.

Creative development

★ Make snow-shakers in plastic bottles. Try various 'snows', such as coconut, rice, plastic chips and glitter.

★ Using pieces of white paper of differing shades, thickness and texture, invite the children to cut out shapes and to layer them to make a winter picture.

★ Look at the clouds and ask the children to imagine what they resemble.

Early years wishing well: Colours and shapes

Look at shapes

(Action rhyme)

Look at the shape of my fingers   (wiggle fingers about)

Look at the shape of my nose   (point to nose)

Look at the shape of my arms and legs   (shake arms and legs)

Look at the shape of my toes   (point to toes)

Look at the shape of an elephant   (wave arm around like a trunk)

Look at the shape of a tree   (spread arms like a tree)

Look at the shape of a tiny mouse   (curl up small)

Then look at the shape of me!   (jump up spreading arms and legs outwards)

Brenda Williams

Early years wishing well: Colours and shapes

Personal, social and emotional development

★ Invite the children to cut and display pictures of noses from old magazines. Ask them to work out which nose you are looking at by asking questions about shape, colour and size, to which you can answer only 'yes' or 'no'. Then, encourage each child in turn to choose a nose while the others ask questions.

★ Share ideas about what we do with our noses. Help the children to understand the need for good hygiene, blowing noses, washing hands, and putting used tissues in the bin. Ask them to make and display posters to help everyone remember these rules.

Communication, language and literacy

★ Invite the children to think about different ways we use our arms and legs and to cut out pictures from magazines to support their suggestions. Mount the pictures with captions on paper cut into arm and leg shapes.

★ Using different examples, show the children how a book has a cover with a title and pages inside. Invite them to make their shaped pages (above) into an arm book and a leg book by fastening the pages together inside a card cover. Encourage them to think of a title for each book.

Mathematical development

★ Help the children to draw around both their hands onto card. Number the fingers from one to ten and use them for counting activities.

★ Draw around the children's feet and colour each pair in stripes, spots or patterns. Cut them out and use for sorting, matching and counting activities.

Knowledge and understanding of the world

★ Using photographs and soft toys, discuss the differences between the life and habitat of a field mouse and those of an elephant.

★ Encourage the children to study their own faces carefully using hand mirrors, and to talk about different characteristics such as hair and skin colour, freckles and glasses.

Physical development

★ Learn a finger rhyme where the fingers are used to make a shape, such as 'Here is a Tree' from *Word Play, Finger Play* (*Play Activities* series, Pre-school Learning Alliance).

★ Make tiny play-dough mice, rolling ball and sausage shapes for the body and tail.

Creative development

★ Draw outlines around the children lying in different shapes on large sheets of paper and invite them to fill in the shapes in broad concentric stripes of bright paint colours.

★ Encourage the children to use elephant, tree and mouse templates to paint silhouettes in colours of their choice. Display these with the stripy cut-outs of children (above).

Painting patterns

Yellow paint to make some twirls

Fill it in with reddish swirls.

Now a stripe and then a dash

Make a dot with every splash.

Wavy lines in red and blue

Lots of squares and circles too.

Paint some diamonds in a row

Watch our pattern really grow!

Brenda Williams

Painting patterns

Personal, social and emotional development

★ Invite the children to work together on a large-scale pattern using a variety of media and materials. Ask the children to take turns to add their section and encourage the whole group to discuss how the next piece of the pattern should be done. Make a note of what each child did and add their names by the relevant sections of the completed mounted picture, with a heading such as, 'Our colourful pattern'.

Communication, language and literacy

★ Collect examples of Morse code, Braille and road signs, and use them to introduce the idea that communication can involve patterns and symbols instead of words.
★ Extend the children's vocabulary by talking about things that twirl and swirl such as leaves, the wind, dancers and Catherine wheels.

Mathematical development

★ Potato-print rows of diamonds. Suggest the children start with one at the top, two in the next row and so on, so that the edge of the pattern looks like a staircase. Together, count the prints in each row.
★ Ask the children to decorate number shapes cut out of card with wavy lines and swirls. Cut the shapes into pieces to make numeral jigsaws for the children to complete.

★ Make repeating patterns using combinations of stripes, dashes and dots.

Knowledge and understanding of the world

★ Go for a walk and look for things in rows, such as houses or plants in a garden.
★ Splash in puddles or drop things into a water tray and watch the pattern of the ripples.

Physical development

★ Encourage the children to make wavy lines in a tray of wallpaper paste coloured blue with paint. Lay a sheet of paper on top and take a print. When dry, paint on squares and circles to make boats, fish and weed.
★ Pretend to be leaves twirling and swirling in the wind, without touching another person.
★ Ask the children to arrange themselves to make 'people patterns', such as lying down straight with their hands touching in a middle point, or standing and crouching alternately in a line.

Creative development

★ Help the children to make splash paintings using a colour of their choice. Invite them to use a contrasting colour to draw wavy lines around the bigger blobs.
★ On a rainy day, suggest that the children make dash patterns with a silver wax crayon over a sheet of white paper to represent rain. Paint over with a grey colour wash, and glue on Cellophane puddles.

Early years wishing well: Colours and shapes

Shape that dough

(Action rhyme)

Roll roll the play dough
(pretend to roll dough in both hands)
See what you can make

First a curly caterpillar
(make wavy movements with hand)
Then a long thin snake
(hold finger towards thumb to indicate thinness then move hand across in straight line)
Curve it in a circle
(draw big circle in the air)
Add some eyes and nose
(pretend to make it into a face by adding eyes and nose)

Squeeze it, squash it, shape it
(pretend to squeeze, squash and shape dough)
That's the way it goes

Roll it in your fingers
(pretend to roll dough in fingers)
To shape a funny mouse
(curl up like a mouse)

A square and a triangle
(draw a square in the air, then a triangle above)
Will make a little house

Roll out the play dough
(pretend to roll play dough in your hands)
See what you can make

Roll it in a little ball
(pretend to make a ball, pass from one hand to the other)
Then flatten it for a cake.
(hold out one hand then clap down the other hand to flatten cake)

Brenda Williams

Shape that dough

Personal, social and emotional development

★ Encourage persistence, curiosity and independence by setting up a 'dough challenge', with a prize of a small bag of play dough for each child. Provide a quiet area, play dough and laminated copies of the photocopiable sheet on page 89 and invite the children to try to make the shapes shown. Allow them to make several attempts until they are satisfied with the result.

★ Hold a special circle time to present the bags of play dough, and for the children to share with each other the shapes they have made.

Communication, language and literacy

★ Make bread with the children and take pictures of the main stages. Talk through the pictures and sequence them with the children, adding captions with key words such as, 'Kneading the dough' and 'Baking the bread'.

★ Make salt-dough plaques. Roll the dough flat and use cutters to make discs, stars and so on. Help the children to add the first letter of their name using worms of dough. Bake the shapes and when they are cool, invite the children to paint the letter and the background different colours. Varnish when the paint has dried.

Mathematical development

★ Using play dough and different-sized square biscuit cutters, ask the children to make a set of 'biscuits' and then arrange them in size order.

★ Make a play-dough snake. Can the children make ones that are fatter, thinner, longer or shorter than the original?

★ Challenge the children to balance a set of bucket scales using play dough.

Knowledge and understanding of the world

★ Make bread dough and 'squeeze it, squash it, shape it' before proving. Once it has risen, bake it, let it cool and eat it!

★ Using salt dough, make small eggs, caterpillars, cocoons and butterflies. Bake and varnish them, and use them to sequence the life cycle of a butterfly.

Physical development

★ Sing the rhyme 'Pat-a-cake, Pat-a-cake, Baker's man', joining in with the hand actions.

Creative development

★ Make salt-dough garlands to give as presents. Encourage each child to roll dough into sausages, join the ends together to make a circle and decorate it with small dough shapes. Bake all the garlands and allow them to cool down before painting and varnishing them.

★ Show the children how to make a house using a paper triangle and a paper square and invite them to add doors and windows with felt-tipped pens. Encourage them to use the paper shapes to create other items, such as a tree or a cat, and to add details with felt-tipped pens.

The shell

(Action rhyme)

Swirly, whirly, twirly shell,   *(spiral motion with hand)*

Are you happy? Who can tell?

Do you wish that you were square,   *(draw square in the air)*

Gently rounded like a pear,   *(cup hands)*

Sharp and pointed like a star?   *(twinkle with hand)*

I like the way you are!

Sue Cowling

Early years wishing well: Colours and shapes

The shell

Personal, social and emotional development

★ Pass a beautiful shell around explaining that something lovely like this can make you feel happy. Encourage the children to talk about what makes them happy, holding the shell while the other children listen and ask questions. Prompt them if necessary with your own suggestions, such as sunsets.

★ Talk to the children about the dangers of sharp and pointed objects, such as scissors, knives and needles. Invite them to think of ways these could be used and stored safely to prevent injury to themselves and others.

Communication, language and literacy

★ Invite the children to try saying the tongue-twister, 'She sells sea shells on the sea-shore'.

★ Ask the children to draw pictures of things beginning with 'sh'. Hang them up in a spiral and watch them twirl around.

★ Cut large sheets of paper into shell, pear and star shapes. Encourage the children to find words that rhyme with each shape and write on their suggestions.

Mathematical development

★ Use shells for sorting, weighing, counting and pattern-making.

★ Make enlarged copies of the photocopiable sheet on page 90 and invite the children to colour in the stars, cut them up and count the points on each shape.

★ Take pairs of shells of different types. Stick one set onto card, place the other set in a box. Ask the children to take a shell out of the box and match it to the shell on the card.

Knowledge and understanding of the world

★ Place a shell to a child's ear and ask if they can hear the sea. Discuss different types of beach: have any of the children ever been to a pebble beach? Did the waves sound different from those on a sandy beach?

★ Compare the colour, taste and texture of raw pears and cooked pears.

★ Using books and photographs, introduce the idea that a shell is a home and offers protection to land and water creatures. Watch garden snails moving in and out of their shells.

Physical development

★ Sing 'If You're Happy and You Know It'. Introduce new verses based on the poem, such as '…Eat a pear'.

★ Invite the children to roll out air-drying clay to about 1cm thick and cut it into a shell shape. Decorate by pressing shells into the clay.

Creative development

★ Make pointed stars from different materials. Try art straws, drinking straws, pipe-cleaners and card.

★ Print with pears that have been cut in half and notice the gently rounded edges that they make.

Early years wishing well: Colours and shapes

Tidying up

The tables in our room
Are not very wide.
Rectangles fit together,
So put them side by side.

Knock down the tower,
Made with building blocks.
Each fits beside the other,
In a big square box.

Take the largest pot,
Then pick up the rest.
The small ones fit inside it,
And make a tidy nest.

Put all the triangles,
And the music things away.
Ready to play, on
Another nursery day.

If we were all more tidy,
And didn't make a muddle,
It would be much easier,
And save a lot of trouble.

Jan Pollard

Early years wishing well: Colours and shapes

Tidying up

Personal, social and emotional development

★ Discuss different ways of helping to tidy up at home. Ask the children to suggest a tidying-up activity that they could do for one week, perhaps putting away toys or placing dirty clothes in the linen basket.

★ Ask the children to help you devise a tidying-up rota for your setting, allocating jobs for the week to groups of children. Make simple certificates on the computer and award one to each child at the end of a successful week.

Communication, language and literacy

★ Design labels for storage boxes. Provide catalogues to cut relevant pictures from, such as toys or stationery. Stick them onto the boxes with a written description where appropriate and cover with sticky-backed plastic.

★ Listen to the song 'Whistle While You Work' from the film *Snow White and the Seven Dwarfs* (Disney). Encourage suggestions on what needs doing at the end of a session and write a jingle to sing while tidying up.

Mathematical development

★ Encourage the children to look for rectangles while playing in the home corner (surfaces, food packaging, furniture). Can they find the long and short sides of the different rectangles and count the corners?

★ Ask the children to find out how many blocks are needed to fill boxes of various sizes.

★ Compare the number of blocks a box will hold when they are thrown in with the number when they are placed carefully.

Knowledge and understanding of the world

★ Find rectangular brick, paving and tile patterns in the local environment and help the children to take rubbings. Encourage them to look at the way rectangles fit together without a gap.

Physical development

★ Use air-drying clay to make pots for storing small items in. Cut out a circular base and demonstrate how to coil long thin sausages of clay on top, sticking the layers together with water to reach the desired height.

★ Help the children to build towers from bricks. Invite them to roll a ball to try and knock them down! Build two towers with a space between them – can the children roll the ball through the gap?

Creative development

★ Make a set of cards showing circles, triangles and rectangles and choose a selection of percussion instruments in these shapes, such as drums, tambourines, triangles and wood blocks. Ask the children to play their instrument when you show the card with the same shape on it. As they gain confidence, display the cards in a row and point to each in turn.

Early years wishing well: Colours and shapes

Triangles

There's a triangle I sit on.
It's a triangle I like.
It's there in the middle
Of my new red bike.

There's a triangle I play on.
It dangles from a string.
When I tap it lightly
It makes a little ting.

There's a climbing frame of triangles.
They make a kind of stair.
I like to scramble up it
And dangle in the air.

There are triangles of fabric
That fill me with delight.
They sail up in the windy sky.
They're on my flying kite.

But the triangles I really think
Are the best by far...
They're the triangles you get inside
A fancy chocolate bar!

Tony Mitton

Early years wishing well: Colours and shapes

Personal, social and emotional development

★ Having counted the pieces, wrap up a triangular chocolate bar in layers of paper, with a paper triangle for each child between each layer. Play 'Pass the parcel' ensuring each child gets a turn. Swap the children's paper triangles for a piece of chocolate at the end. (**NB** Check for possible food allergies).

Communication, language and literacy

★ Ask the children to imagine that they are riding on a giant kite. What would they see as they flew higher and higher? Record their ideas and attach their pictures and writing onto kite shapes and display them ascending up the wall.

Mathematical development

★ Give the children some paint and triangular sponges and ask them to sponge-print diamond kite shapes. Encourage them to try to fit several triangles together to make larger kites.

★ Use the sponges to print tails of different lengths for the kites. Help the children to print tails made up of between one and ten triangles. Add that number to the kite and display all the kites together as a number line.

Knowledge and understanding of the world

★ Hold a 'Bicycle day'. Look at the shape of the frame, the saddle and the wheels of a bicycle. Talk about wearing a helmet and riding bicycles safely. Display photographs of old-fashioned bicycles.

★ Show the children photographs from books such as *Summer* (*Festivals through the Year* series, Heinemann), and share information about Kodomono-hi, the Japanese children's festival, when kites are flown.

Physical development

★ Invite the children to pedal a bicycle or a tricycle between two triangles drawn on the ground. Mark each corner of the smaller triangle with cones and ask the children to park their vehicles carefully inside it.

★ Ask the children to cut the corners off a paper equilateral triangle. Can they fit the straight edges of these pieces together to make a new shape?

★ Visit a playground and look for triangular shapes on the equipment. Talk about playing safely before encouraging the children to 'scramble and dangle'!

Creative development

★ Use percussion triangles to investigate loud and soft sounds. Sing 'I Hear Thunder', in *This Little Puffin…* compiled by Elizabeth Matterson (Puffin Books), and make soft sounds for the raindrops and harder repeated sounds for the thunder.

★ Use art straws to make triangles of different sizes. Display them, hanging one inside another, fastened to a triangular coat hanger. Watch them move and turn in the air.

Drawing shapes

(Action rhyme)

Draw a circle *(draw shape of circle in the air)*

Round and round *(keep drawing round and round)*

Roll the circle *(pretend to put the circle on the ground and roll it)*

On the ground.

Draw a square *(draw a square in the air)*

In the air

Draw four legs *(pretend to add four legs)*

And it's a chair. *(pretend to take it out of the air and sit on it)*

Draw a triangle *(draw a triangle in the air)*

With three sides

Like a roof *(places hands over head to form an apex)*

Where you can hide. *(stoop slightly with hands still forming roof)*

Brenda Williams

Early years wishing well: Colours and shapes

Drawing shapes

Personal, social and emotional development

★ Encourage the children to think about good hiding places for animals and reasons why they might hide. Go outside and look for places where animals might be, such as in holes, under stones, wood and plants. Emphasize the need to leave any creatures where they are found.

★ Ask the group to help sort out a collection of objects into 'can roll' and 'can't roll'. Encourage the children to choose an item in turn, test it and tell the others what they are finding out. Include simple items like an orange or book, and more difficult ones like a coin that can only roll on the edge.

Communication, language and literacy

★ Read *Happy Birthday, Sam* by Pat Hutchins (Bodley Head), a story where a boy gets a chair for a present.

★ Using pictures and examples, introduce vocabulary for different parts of a chair and different types of chairs.

★ Find out if the children have a favourite chair or place to sit and talk about why these places are special.

Mathematical development

★ Give the children opportunities to draw shapes in different ways – in the air, in sand, in shaving foam, with paint, glue and glitter and with sticks in mud.

★ Decorate a large circle by drawing on smaller circles, squares and triangles. Mark a dice with these shapes. Ask the children to take turns to roll the dice and colour in a corresponding shape on the picture.

Knowledge and understanding of the world

★ Copy the photocopiable sheet on page 91 onto A3 paper. Give the children catalogues and ask them to find and cut out different types of furniture with four legs to stick in the different rooms in the house.

★ Make triangle-cut sandwiches or samosas with the children, hiding the fillings inside.

Physical development

★ Play a game of 'Musical chairs'.

★ Invite the children to roll around the floor, changing direction, speed and shape, without bumping into one another.

Creative development

★ Working with the children, use a selection of sheets, blankets, thick rope, chairs, climbing frame, or trees to make triangular tents to hide in.

★ Show the children how to draw around a circle onto paper and cut it out. Encourage them to make their own paper disc and then to draw a triangle, cut it out and stick one of its corners to the disc to make a fish. Finally, ask them to decorate their fish shapes with collage materials.

Chocolate choice

Tom loved visiting his Grandma. Her house was always warm and there was a brilliant view across the valley from the back window. But best of all, Gran always had a box of chocolates that she kept hidden in a different place for Tom to find.

One day, before it was time for Tom to go home, Gran told Tom to look in the drawer where she kept her pens and pencils. Tom opened the drawer in the bureau and there was a box of chocolates!

'Bring the box over here, Tom, and let's have one each!' said Gran.

Tom carried the box carefully to his Gran and watched while she took off the Cellophane wrapper and lifted the lid.

'Mmm!' said Tom, as the delicious smell of chocolates wafted from the box. 'Chocolatey! Lovely!'

'Pick your favourite, Tom,' said Gran.

Tom peered at the chocolates. They were all the same colour – a rich, dark, shiny brown – but they were all different shapes.

Round ones, square ones, triangles and ovals, smooth ones and lumpy ones. Some had chocolate swirls and patterns on the top. Which one was his favourite? Tom liked the look of the round one. But the triangle looked good, too. And then there was that square one...

'There's a picture of them inside the lid, to tell us what they all are,' said Gran.

'What's in that round one, Gran?' asked Tom.

'That's a strawberry cream,' said Gran.

'What about the triangle one?'

'That's a coffee cream,' said Gran.

'And what's the square one?' asked Tom.

'That's orange-flavoured chocolate,' said Gran. 'They're all delicious. Which one would you like, Tom?'

Tom thought very hard and tried to imagine all the different flavours. At last, he picked out the round, strawberry cream and popped it into his mouth.

'Mmm! Scrummy!' he said.

Gran laughed. 'Well, I'm going to have the coffee cream. It's a good job we have the pictures to help us choose!'

The next time Tom went to visit his Gran, he had a special surprise for her. When Gran went into the kitchen to make the tea, Tom put a box on the table.

'Oh,' said Gran, when she saw the box. 'What's this?'

'Open it up and see!' said Tom, grinning.

Gran opened the box. 'Ooh, lovely! Home-made biscuits to have with our tea! Did you help to make them, Tom?'

'Yes,' said Tom. 'And they're special biscuits. There are three flavours and this will help you choose which one to have.'

He handed Gran a piece of paper. Tom had made a special drawing of a round biscuit, a triangle-shaped biscuit and a square biscuit. It showed her that the round ones were strawberry-flavoured, the square ones were orange-flavoured, and the triangle-shaped ones were coffee-flavoured.

'What fun!' said Gran, looking closely at Tom's drawing. Then she chose her favourite – the coffee-flavoured, triangle-shaped one!

Davey Moore

Early years wishing well: Colours and shapes

Chocolate choice

Personal, social and emotional development

★ Hide a box containing the children's name cards in a different place each day. Give small groups of children responsibility for finding it.

Communication, language and literacy

★ Ask the children to choose a biscuit from a selection box, following the key to the different types. Encourage each child to describe the flavour and texture of their biscuit as they eat it. Does the biscuit match its description?
★ Share the poem 'Chocolate Milkshake' from *Poems for the Very Young* edited by Michael Rosen (Kingfisher Books). Point out the 'noisy' words such as 'glug', 'slurp', 'gurgle' and 'plop'. Invite the children to help you to write a poem about a chocolate biscuit using the same format. What noises might be heard while making and eating it?

Mathematical development

★ Randomly number each compartment of several matching chocolate-box liners from one to ten and give one liner to each child in a small group. Call out numbers and ask the children to place a button in the corresponding compartment. The first child to fill their liner must shout 'chocolate!'.
★ Make chocolate biscuits. Help the children to weigh the ingredients, cut out different shapes and time the baking.

Knowledge and understanding of the world

★ Let the children feel a wrapped bar of chocolate. Let them watch as you melt the unwrapped chocolate bar and pour it into a small jelly mould. Talk about how it has changed, what might happen to it if you put it in the fridge and what shape it will be.
★ Show the children the recycling codes on the bottom of a plastic chocolate-box liner. Talk about the importance of recycling plastic, glass, paper and metal.

Physical development

★ Using salt dough, ask the children to make different-shaped 'biscuits' and bake them. When they are cool, decorate them with swirls and patterns. Encourage the children to use them in role-play and for the following game.
★ Invite the children to help take the 'biscuits' from the oven (cardboard box) to a basket on the opposite side of the room. Introduce different ways of moving such as hopping, running or jumping, to collect a biscuit. Ask the children to sit down when their biscuit is in the basket.

Creative development

★ Make a group mobile using foil chocolate-wrappers to decorate cardboard shapes. Fasten the shapes to a card rectangle, decorated to look like a chocolate bar, and hang the mobile up.

The Russian doll

Abigail loved her dolls. She liked to push them up and down the hall in the doll's pram, or dress them up in different clothes. And she liked them to sleep in her bed at night.

But one day, Abigail's uncle brought her a very strange doll that he had bought while he was on holiday. It was a Russian doll. She was made of wood and she had a painted face, a painted red dress and headscarf, and painted arms and legs. Abigail was not sure that she really liked her, but she thanked her uncle for his present.

'Call her Ivanna,' said Abigail's uncle. 'It's a Russian name.'

Abigail tried to put Ivanna in her doll's pram, but she would not sit up because her legs were only painted ones. When Abigail pushed the pram along the hall, Ivanna slipped down under the cover.

'You're a silly doll,' said Abigail.

That night, Abigail took Ivanna to bed. But in the middle of the night, Abigail woke up with something very hard sticking into her back. It was Ivanna.

'You're a silly doll,' said Abigail.

The next day was very cold. Abigail sorted through her doll's clothes and found a woollen top for Ivanna. She put it over Ivanna's head, but it slipped right down and fell off because Ivanna's arms were only painted ones.

'You're a silly doll,' said Abigail.

Abigail's mum called up the stairs, 'Have you put warm clothes on today, Abigail?'

'Yes, I have,' said Abigail. 'But Ivanna hasn't. She has to wear the same things all the time.'

'No, she doesn't,' said Abigail's mum coming into the bedroom. 'She has lots of clothes. Look.'

She held Ivanna in both hands and twisted. Ivanna's top half came right off, and inside Abigail saw a smaller Ivanna, wearing a dress in a different colour.

Then Abigail's mum took out the smaller doll and twisted it. Inside was an even smaller Ivanna, wearing another dress! Abigail was amazed.

Mum carried on twisting and pulling, until there were five different Ivannas altogether.

'Five Ivannas!' said Abigail. 'And all wearing different colours!' She stood them up in a row.

'You're a very clever doll, Ivanna,' said Abigail.

Barbara Ball

Early years wishing well: Colours and shapes

The Russian doll

Personal, social and emotional development

★ Play 'Pass the parcel' with a Russian doll, removing a doll and placing it in the centre each time the music is stopped, until the tiny doll is revealed. Play again, building the doll back up.

★ Let the children talk about their own special toys. Read *Dogger* by Shirley Hughes (Red Fox) which is about a favourite toy that gets lost. Talk about how we can look after toys.

Communication, language and literacy

★ Learn the rhyme 'Miss Polly Had a Dolly', in *This Little Puffin…* compiled by Elizabeth Matterson (Puffin Books).

★ Collect dolls made from plastic, wood, cloth, and metal. Draw their outlines onto large sheets of paper. Ask the children to examine the dolls, suggesting words to describe them. Scribe these around the corresponding outline. Read the words and ask individual children to match the dolls to the sheets.

Mathematical development

★ Make five different-sized 'Ivanna' dolls from card. Ask the children to paint each one a different colour and number them. Use them for work on size order, number line activities and to illustrate the counting rhyme 'There Were Five in the Bed'.

Knowledge and understanding of the world

★ Ask parents and carers to send in mementoes of a holiday or a day out and display these next to a map of either the UK or the world, depending on the items. Make a line between the mementoes and the places with wool.

★ Hold a 'Russia' day looking at photographs (from travel books) of people, places and the weather. Cook and eat Russian food, such as blinis, and invite the children to listen and dance to Russian music.

Physical development

★ Help the children to make a string of paper dolls, folding up a long strip of paper and cutting out a doll shape with the hand and the foot extending to the folded edge.

★ Encourage the children to practise making twisting actions, by using wind-up toys, plastic bottles with lids, and nuts and bolts while playing.

Creative development

★ Invite the children to make small dolls from wooden dolly pegs, adding fabric clothes and wool hair.

★ Turn the role-play area into a holiday corner where children can play at 'holidays'. Provide travel brochures, chairs to become transport, and a stall to buy holiday souvenirs and postcards.

A day at the fair

Laura and Timmy were very excited. They were going to visit the fairground for the first time, with their Aunt Sue and Uncle Ross.

'What do we do at the fair?' asked Laura.

'We all have fun – you'll see!' smiled Uncle Ross.

The first thing they noticed was the noise! And the colour! Laura and Timmy didn't know where to look first. They kept tight hold of Aunt Sue's hands. Uncle Ross bought some tickets so they could go on the rides. 'Can we go on that slide?' asked Laura, pointing to a tall slide that curved round and round like a huge wriggly spiral.

'Of course,' said Uncle Ross. 'That's the helter-skelter.'

They picked up a mat each, and then they climbed up the steps right to the top. They sat on their mats and slid all the way down the spirally slide. Round and round they went. Down and down and down. Faster and faster.

Laura and Timmy yelled all the way.

'Now let's see if we can win a prize at the hoopla stall,' said Aunt Sue. 'You have to throw a ring over something to win a prize.' Timmy was too small to throw a hoop, but they all cheered when Aunt Sue 'looped' a big teddy bear.

'Hall of Mirrors next!' said Uncle Ross, striding off. Laura and Timmy hurried to keep up.

The walls inside the Hall of Mirrors were lined with different-shaped mirrors. Some were square, some were round, some were tall and thin, and some were wavy.

Reflections became funny-shaped, too. 'Look! I'm a wiggly worm!' said Timmy.

'Oh, I'm short and fat!' shrieked Laura.

'I'm as round as a ball!' laughed Aunt Sue. 'Look at my tiny head!'

'I'm like a lamppost!' said Uncle Ross.

They laughed until their sides hurt.

'Time for a ride on the Big Wheel!' said Uncle Ross. It looked enormous! Timmy was a bit scared at first, but Aunt Sue held on tight to him and he soon began to enjoy himself. Up, up, up they went, then down, down, down. It was brilliant.

They just had time to ride on the roundabout, with its colourful, prancing horses, when it was time to go home.

'Did you enjoy that?' asked Uncle Ross as he drove them home in the car.

But there was no reply: Laura and Timmy were fast asleep!

Karen King

Early years wishing well: Colours and shapes

A day at the fair

Personal, social and emotional development

★ Challenge groups of children to a treasure hunt. Hide different ring-shaped objects around the setting for them to collect, such as a swimming-ring, a bagel, a mint, a doughnut or pictures showing the letter 'o'.

★ Talk about busy, noisy places that the children have visited, such as shopping centres. Ask how they felt and why the children in the story kept tight hold of their aunt's hands. Talk about staying close to an adult and what the children should do if they did ever become lost.

Communication, language and literacy

★ Encourage the children to make up a fairground song to the tune of 'What Shall We Do with the Drunken Sailor' changing the words to 'What shall we do when we go to the fairground?', with the last line beginning with phrases such as, 'We'll ride on the…' or 'We will win a…'.

★ Using information books about fairgrounds for inspiration, ask small groups of children to make up short 'What am I?' riddles for different rides and sideshows. For instance, a roundabout might be, 'Round and round, up and down, hold on tight!'. Encourage the children to draw a picture to accompany their riddle and scribe the words onto a separate piece of paper for them. Fasten it onto the corresponding picture to form a lift-up flap. Make the pictures and captions into a book.

Mathematical development

★ Use an enlarged copy on card of the photocopiable sheet on page 92 to make number jigsaws. Show the children the completed jigsaws, then jumble them up. The children must roll corresponding numbers on a dice in order to add the pieces to complete the jigsaws.

★ Use large game hoops during sorting activities to place sets of objects inside.

Knowledge and understanding of the world

★ Using flexible plastic mirrors and large metal spoons, encourage the children to explore the different 'funny-shaped' reflections of their face.

Physical development

★ Make a hoopla game with small prizes such as stickers or raisins.

★ Ask the children to draw a spiral onto a card disc and cut along it with scissors. Lay the spirals flat and invite the children to decorate them with glitter, hang them up and watch them going around.

Creative development

★ Invite the children to make a fairground from junk materials and use it with small-world people.

★ Learn the song 'The Animal Fair' from *Okki-Tokki-Unga* edited by Beatrice Harrop (A&C Black).

Early years wishing well: Colours and shapes

My finger puppet

The last time we went to visit my Auntie Hyacinth, my brother Winston went off to play with my cousin Jonah on their skateboards and Auntie and I made finger puppets together.

First, Auntie got out this huge bag from her cupboard. It was her sewing bag, full of pieces of fabric and trimmings left over from her dressmaking.

Auntie asked me what kind of puppet I'd like to make. I had to think a bit: I'd already got a duck, a crocodile, a penguin and a donkey. I decided to make a butterfly.

We looked at the pieces of fabric from Auntie's sewing bag, and I chose a square of bright yellow felt.

Aunt Hyacinth folded the square in half and made it into a rectangle. Then she shook her head and opened it up again. This time she folded the square so that it made a triangle.

I took a felt pen and drew a wing shape on the fold of the triangle where Auntie showed me. We cut round the wing shape and when the felt was flattened out again, there were two wings exactly the same and joined together in the middle!

Next Auntie reached into her sewing bag and brought out a heart-shaped tin full of tiny round sequins of every colour. I chose silver and blue ones. Auntie showed me how to glue them carefully onto the wings of the butterfly. I wanted to make a diamond pattern, but they were too fiddly and sticky!

There was just enough yellow felt left for the butterfly's body. Auntie cut out two long oval shapes, a bit fatter and longer than my finger, and sewed them together leaving the bottom open.

I put my butterfly on my finger and took it outside for a fly around in the sun. The little wings flapped and sparkled brilliantly.

When Winston came back, he thought my finger puppet was really cool. He wondered if Aunt Hyacinth would make him a scary spider for his skateboard!

Geraldine Taylor

Early years wishing well: Colours and shapes

My finger puppet

Personal, social and emotional development

★ Invite the children to paint happy and sad faces onto two small paper plates; fasten them together with a lolly stick sandwiched in-between. Sit in a circle with the children and ask them, 'How do you feel today?'. Explain that they should turn their puppet to show you the appropriate face. Encourage them to share with the group their reasons for feeling this way.

★ Talk about times when family members share special skills with a child, such as baking or football.

Communication, language and literacy

★ Use a crocodile puppet (a green sock with felt teeth and eyes) and appropriate objects to play sound games. Give the children an initial or end sound to listen for. The crocodile selects objects and the children shout 'snap' if the word starts or ends with the chosen sound – for example, for 't', a cat would get a snap but a duck would not.

★ Encourage the children to make up and re-enact stories using puppets.

Mathematical development

★ Make shape pop-up puppets by fastening dowelling rods to different card shapes and concealing them inside covered cereal boxes that have had the bottom and top removed. With the children watching, slowly push up a shape puppet. How quickly can they guess the shape before it is fully revealed?

★ Challenge the children to fold squares of paper to make rectangles and triangles. Ask them to decorate these with matching potato-print shapes.

Knowledge and understanding of the world

★ Display different types of puppets such as string, finger, stick, pop-up and glove puppets. Encourage the children to play with them and make them move.

Physical development

★ Encourage the children to 'walk' their first two fingers along a surface. Show them this movement with a hand puppet and invite them to make their own version by cutting out an oval of card and decorating it using felt-tipped pens to resemble a person or creature. Help them to cut holes for the fingers and let them make their puppets walk.

Creative development

★ Invite the children to make a spider puppet by painting a paper cup black. Help the children to cut eight holes around the open end and thread black pipe-cleaners through them. Turn the cup upside down and fasten elastic cord to the top so it will bounce up and down.

★ Invite the children to make a felt butterfly finger puppet as described in the text.

63

What's in the parcel?

Last week, my friend Nasreen had a birthday. Mrs Flynn, our nursery teacher, brought in some cakes and fruit drinks so we could have a party, and we played several games.

One of them was a guessing game. We had a sack full of funny-shaped parcels, and we had to guess what was in them. Some of the regular shapes had names. The box, for instance, which Nasreen pulled from the sack, had sides that were all the same size. Mrs Flynn said it was a **cube**. Just like a very large sugar lump!

Nasreen shook her parcel to see if it rattled. She thought very hard about what it could be. Then she said she thought it was a box of tissues.

Mrs Flynn told her to unwrap her parcel – and there was a square box of pink tissues!

Clever Nasreen.

Then it was Oliver's turn to choose. His parcel was a long, round tube. Mrs Flynn called it a **cylinder**. When Oliver shook the parcel, it made a shuffly, rattly sort of noise. He guessed it was a tube of his favourite kind of potato crisps. And he was right.

Leon's parcel was completely round. This one was called a **sphere**. It was easy to guess, as it bounced when he dropped it on the floor. We all shouted out that it was a ball!

Angela had a very light parcel. At first she thought there was nothing in it! Then she

thought about its funny shape: it was round at the bottom, and pointed at the top. Just like a...*party hat!* Angela unwrapped the hat and put it on her head. Mrs Flynn called it a **cone**.

There were just two parcels left: one for Pat and one for me. Pat's parcel was long, with three straight sides. It was called a **prism**. Everyone guessed that it was going to be a scrummy chocolate bar!

My parcel wasn't at all regular. It had no straight sides, but it wasn't rounded. Instead it was very lumpy and squashy. I felt it carefully all over. I poked it and shook it. What could it be? Something soft, with a round lumpy bit at the top, and four sticky-out bits at the sides...

Everyone in the class was waiting for me to say what I thought it was!

Then I guessed it was...a teddy bear.

I quickly unwrapped the parcel and a furry, cuddly teddy-bear face looked out of the crumpled paper.

Did teddy bears have a shape-name? Mrs Flynn said they were called teddy bears – and we all giggled.

It was a good game, and afterwards we shared out the crisps and chocolates, and gave Nasreen the other things as presents for her birthday!

Jackie Andrews

What's in the parcel?

Personal, social and emotional development

★ Play a similar guessing game to the one in the story, changing the objects in the parcels.

★ Talk about how birthdays are a reminder of the day we were born. Using information books and artefacts from resource centres, find out how different cultures celebrate birth, welcoming the child and giving it a name.

★ Hold a class party where everyone helps to make simple food and decorations.

Communication, language and literacy

★ Read *Kipper's Birthday* by Mick Inkpen (Hodder) and talk about why his friends came on the wrong day.

★ Collect examples of invitations for birthdays, weddings and celebrations, and look at the wording on them. Provide a basic template and ask the children to make an invitation to give to another child, inviting them to a class party. Encourage them to place the invitations into named envelopes and to deliver them.

Mathematical development

★ Fill three small identical boxes with varying amounts of rice to make them different weights, and wrap each one in different paper. Ask the children to find the heaviest and the lightest by holding them. Use balance scales to check whether their estimations were correct.

★ Ask the children to make a 'birthdays calendar' by cutting 12 large parcel shapes from wrapping paper (they could use their hand-decorated paper, see 'Creative development') and labelling them with the months of the year. Attach ribbon to the parcels and invite each child to write their name on a label and to tie it to the month corresponding to their birthday. Then ask the children to display the parcels in a row in month order.

Knowledge and understanding of the world

★ Show the children different types of potato-based snacks and crisps and invite them to make their own. Cut thin slices of potato with a vegetable peeler and let the children stamp out shapes with cutters. Brush with oil and bake until crisp.

Physical development

★ Play party games with the children such as 'Musical statues' and 'Pass the parcel'.

Creative development

★ Invite each child to make their own wrapping paper using shaped sponges and paint.

★ Make party hats with the children. Roll pieces of A4 card into cones and secure them. Cut off the excess point at the base of the hat and attach shirring elastic. Encourage the children to decorate their hats with paper shapes, glitter and sequins.

The collage

Today, mum showed me how to make a collage picture. That's a picture made with stuck-on pieces of material and other things, instead of crayons or paints. It's good fun. First, we filled a box with scraps of material, coloured paper, buttons and other odds and ends to glue onto the picture. Then we covered the table with newspaper and put the box, some paste and a brush on top. I put on my apron and we were ready to start.

Mum took a sheet of sugar paper and drew a picture with her pencil of a duck swimming on a lake. I drew the sun and some clouds in the sky. Then Mum showed me how to fill in the different parts of the picture. First, she cut a triangle of yellow felt and pasted it onto the duck's beak. It looked good. I wanted to have a go, too!

Mum said I could cut the paper and materials into any shapes I liked. So I cut some squares of blue paper and green, shiny fabric and glued them over the lake part. I pasted some of the shapes over each other to make sure I filled in all the gaps.

After that, we cut squares and triangles

of material and stuck them all over the duck's body and head. It looked very bright and colourful.

Then I took a round, black button and glued that onto the space for the duck's eye. Next we cut some thin, diamond shapes from green felt and pasted them onto the plants in the lake. I found some flowered material and carefully cut round some of the flower shapes and stuck them over the green leaves. My plants were flowering!

That left the sun, sky and clouds. Mum cut a circle of yellow paper for the sun and I stuck it on. Then we cut lots of oblong shapes from a piece of silky, blue material and stuck them over the sky. Last of all, we cut some white circles and pasted them onto the fluffy white clouds, overlapping them.

It took quite a while to finish our collage. It's much quicker to paint a picture, but not as much fun, and it doesn't have all the pretty patterns that you can get from using different materials.

Karen King

the collage

Personal, social and emotional development

★ Give small groups of children a duck outline, coloured tissue-paper shapes and glue. Ask them to look at photographs of different ducks (from bird magazines) and to choose one that they like. Can they decorate their duck with tissue to resemble the photograph, leaving no gaps?

★ Make card copies of the scissors and glue pot on the photocopiable sheet on page 93. Attach a safety pin securely to the back to make badges for the children. Award these to the children when they show care in performing cutting and gluing skills, and invite each child to show their work to the group.

Communication, language and literacy

★ Place small pieces of collage materials in different textures (fabrics, nylon, pan scrubs, sandpaper, plastic, chipped bark, glitter) in dishes. Invite the children to select a material, describing how it feels and what it reminds them of, before gluing it onto a letter of the alphabet. Use the 'feely' letters for alphabet activities.

Mathematical development

★ Learn the finger rhyme 'Five Little Ducks,' from *This Little Puffin…* compiled by Elizabeth Matterson (Puffin Books) and ask the children to enact the song using one large and five small plastic ducks in a water tray.

★ Ask the children to fill small boxes with fabric scraps so that they are full, half-full and empty.

Knowledge and understanding of the world

★ Visit a local pond or river to observe the ducks, noticing how they swim, dive and feed. Ask for assistance from plenty of adult helpers and ensure that the children are aware of the importance of behaving sensibly and safely.

★ Using photographs from bird magazines and books, talk about the life cycle of a duck. Encourage the children to look closely at where the eggs are laid and the differences between the duckling and the adult.

Physical development

★ Help the children to cut a flower shape out of felt and sew it to a rectangle of felt using large running stitches along the centre of each petal. Sew a button onto the centre of the flower to finish. Glue onto thick card to make a picture.

Creative development

★ As a group, make a four-season collage of a fruit-bearing tree. Use real examples of seeds, leaves and fruit from a local tree and let the children make prints with the leaves, stick seeds to the picture and copy the fruit in their painting. Make a panel each season with the children's work and keep the panels from one season to the other to show how the tree has changed. Each season, display examples of the blossoms, leaves and fruit while they are fresh.

Early years wishing well: Colours and shapes

A great big square

(Tune: 'Girls and Boys Come Out to Play')

I can make a great big square, I'll draw it now up in the air.

See the corn-ers and see the sides of e-qual length both long and wide.

Johanne Levy

Early years wishing well: Colours and shapes

A great big square

Personal, social and emotional development

★ Cut out a large paper square. Ask the children to look for squares in magazines and on packaging to bring in and stick onto the square. Encourage them to tell the group where they found their pieces.

★ Play games that encourage turn-taking and are based on squares, such as 'Snakes and Ladders' or 'Hopscotch'.

Communication, language and literacy

★ Provide squared paper and crayons and challenge the children to try and make the initial letter of their name out of squares.

★ Make a class story-book about a magic square that can become different things. Suggest ideas to inspire the children, such as a flying carpet, a paper aeroplane or a wooden box.

Mathematical development

★ Gather a selection of different squares and encourage the children to count their corners and sides. Ask them if it is always the same number.

★ Use different resources like play dough, ribbons and straws to make sets of things that are equal in length.

★ Invite the children to join together five squares, side to side, each square touching another. How many different shapes can they create?

Knowledge and understanding of the world

★ Make a display showing squares in the environment using packaging, magazine pictures and items such as pieces of chocolate, tiles and CD cases.

★ Ask the children to look at floors and walls for different types of coverings that are made up of squares. Look out for tiles, mosaic, wood block and carpet tiles.

★ Steer a remote control car around a course and park it inside a square.

Physical development

★ Place large card squares of different colours in the four corners of a room. Ask the children to dance to music and, when you call out a colour, to try and reach the corresponding corner before the music stops.

★ Help the children to make sandwiches and cut them into squares to eat.

★ Draw squares of different sizes in the air.

Creative development

★ Use square paper to try some simple origami, following the instructions on the photocopiable sheet on page 94.

★ Collect together items with square sides such as bricks, boxes and pieces of wood, for printing with paint onto square pieces of paper.

★ Help the children to cut large squares from stiff card and cut a slot from the edge to the centre. Slot the squares together to form a 3D sculpture.

Early years wishing well: Colours and shapes

Boxes

(Tune: 'Bobby Shaftoe')

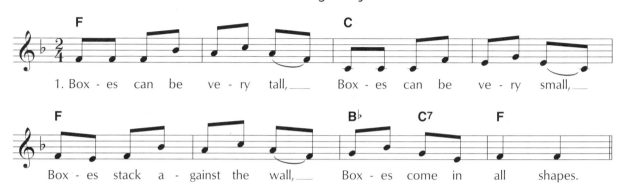

1. Box - es can be ve - ry tall,___ Box - es can be ve - ry small,___
Box - es stack a - gainst the wall,___ Box - es come in all shapes.

2. Boxes can be very wide,
Boxes always have six sides,
Boxes can be great to hide in
Boxes come in all shapes.

3. Boxes made of many things,
Cardboard, metal, paper, tin,
Some tied up with tape or string
Boxes come in all shapes.

Peter Morrell

Early years wishing well: Colours and shapes

Boxes

Personal, social and emotional development

★ Give groups of children a matchbox and challenge them to fit as many different things as possible inside it.

★ Make a 'body parts dice' by gluing pictures of a head, arm, leg, hand, foot and body onto the sides of a large box. Invite the children to take turns to roll the dice and perform an action for the part shown, such as clapping hands, nodding heads or bending knees. Encourage the whole group to join in with the movement.

Communication, language and literacy

★ Make themed story boxes to help develop imaginative stories. Place four items into a box and ask the children to think of a story involving these items. A dinosaur box might include a dinosaur egg, a picture of a cave, an aeroplane and a footprint.

★ Write letters on separate boxes and fill these with items starting with the corresponding letter, so the 'c' box could contain a car, a cat and a crayon.

Mathematical development

★ Hide an object under a set of boxes numbered 1 to 5. Ask the children to guess which box it is under. Introduce more boxes and give clues such as 'higher' or 'lower'.

★ Ask the children to find out how many sides a box has. Provide pens and plenty of boxes and ask the children to number each side as they count them.

★ Challenge the children to find a box that does not have six sides.

Knowledge and understanding of the world

★ Make a montage of magazine pictures showing boxes that are used for different purposes such as storage, lunch, tools, shape-sorting and posting letters. Ask the children to bring in boxes of their choice from home, and display them with the montage as a backing.

★ Fill boxes with materials such as feathers, coins, pasta and rice for the children to shake and feel.

Physical development

★ Learn the action rhyme 'Here is a Box', in *This Little Puffin...* compiled by Elizabeth Matterson (Puffin Books).

★ Invite the children to pretend to be Jack-in-the-boxes being pressed down, then jumping up and wobbling around.

Creative development

★ Open up the ends of several large boxes and cut holes in the sides of others. Join them together to make tunnels and hiding places.

★ Practise wrapping up parcels using a selection of old wrapping paper and different-sized boxes. Create a role-play post office area with scales, stamps and sacks. Deliver the parcels using vans made from boxes.

Early years wishing well: Colours and shapes

Just the same

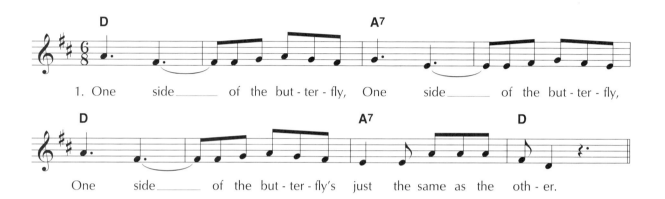

1. One side___ of the but-ter-fly, One side___ of the but-ter-fly,

One side___ of the but-ter-fly's just the same as the oth-er.

2. One side of the teddy bear...

3. One side of the little doll...

4. One side of the little house...

Cut around the pictures of the photocopiable sheet on page 95, cut them in half along the vertical line and use them for matching as you sing the song. The children could make paint-and-fold butterflies.

Susan Eames

Just the same

Personal, social and emotional development

★ Pass a model house around a circle. Invite each child to tell the others what they like about their own home and why.

★ Ask the children to study their own faces in a mirror and notice whether both halves are exactly the same.

Communication, language and literacy

★ Make copies of the photocopiable sheet on page 95. Photocopy the butterfly section onto card and cut it into two, giving each child in a pair one half. Ask them to sit back to back while one child describes how he is colouring in his half and the other tries to colour in her half in the same way. When the children have finished, put the butterfly halves together to see if both sides are the same.

★ Cut out a large butterfly shape and scribe words onto it about butterflies, their colour, pattern and the way they move.

Mathematical development

★ Make copies on card of the photocopiable sheet on page 95. Invite the children to colour in the pictures so that both sides match. Cut them in half and use them to play 'Pairs'.

★ Decorate a box as a wall and cut five brown teddy outlines from card. Sing 'Five Brown Teddies' using the tune 'Five Green Bottles', counting the teddies as they fall off.

★ Give the children an A4 piece of paper with a picture of a butterfly in the centre. Challenge them to draw a smaller butterfly to one side and a bigger one to the other.

Knowledge and understanding of the world

★ Make small cakes with the children. Decorate them to look like teddy faces with chocolate button ears, raisins for the eyes and half a cherry for the nose. Eat them at a teddy bears' picnic.

★ Using photographs, books and dolls sent in or borrowed from a local museum, make a display of dolls through the ages.

Physical development

★ Learn some action rhymes about houses, dolls and teddy bears, such as 'My Little House Won't Stand Up Straight' and 'Teddy Bear, Teddy Bear Touch Your Nose' from *This Little Puffin…* compiled by Elizabeth Matterson (Puffin Books).

★ Stick half of a simple outline drawing, such as a ball, onto paper. Invite the children to draw in the missing half. For a simpler activity, make dotted outlines of the missing part.

Creative development

★ Copy three bear outlines and one doll outline onto card. Ask the children to decorate them using collage materials. Use them to tell the story of 'Goldilocks and the Three Bears'.

Early years wishing well: Colours and shapes

Look for circles

(Tune: 'London Bridge')

1. See the cir - cle shapes we found, shapes we found, shapes we found.

Clocks and wheels and plates are round, Look for cir - cles!

2. See the circle shapes we found,
Shapes we found, shapes we found.
Buttons, hoops and dots are round,
Look for circles!

This can be sung using a collection of round or mixed-shaped objects. The changing third line can be adapted to match those in the collection, for example, 'Badges and CDs are round'; 'Janet's photo frame is round' and so on.

Sue Nicholls

Early years wishing well: Colours and shapes

Personal, social and emotional development

★ Make medals from discs of gold card. Award them for special achievements based on social skills such as helping other children or sharing.

Communication, language and literacy

★ Invite the children to think of other circular objects and help them to write the words on a large circular piece of paper.

★ Make the role-play area into 'Circle Cottage'. Provide crockery, pans, food, hats, spotty clothing, cushions and stools, all involving circles. Encourage the children to make up stories about 'Circle Cottage' and record them using a tape recorder.

Mathematical development

★ Take photographs of the children's activities throughout the day. Mount them in time order around a large card clock-face. Ask carers to send in photographs showing the children's life at home, mealtimes, bedtime and sleeping, to complete the clock, then read the circular 'story' of a child's day.

★ Ask the children to make circular play-dough cakes and place each one on a plate. Invite them to decorate each cake with 'cherries' by rolling a dice and adding the corresponding number of red counters. When all the cakes are decorated, can the children group them in sets by numbers of cherries?

★ Collect interesting buttons from charity shops and old clothing and use them for sorting, matching and counting activities.

Knowledge and understanding of the world

★ Count the wheels on different types of vehicle. Count how many of each vehicle passes your setting in one morning or week. Talk about how the location of your setting might affect the number of vehicles that pass.

★ Make vehicles from construction materials.

★ Send toy cars down a tube and see which travels the furthest.

Physical development

★ Use different-coloured paint to draw concentric circles on circular paper.

★ Introduce singing and dancing games that are performed in circles – *Oranges and Lemons* by Karen King (Oxford University Press) has a good selection.

Creative development

★ Gather together buttons, sequins, baking cases, paper circles and doilies. Use them to make a circles collage.

★ Show the children pointillism artwork by Georges Seurat and Paul Signac, observing carefully the dots of colour carefully placed on the paper. Provide paint and pieces of dowelling and encourage the children to make their own dot pictures. Display these together with the original pointillism artwork.

Patterns

(Tune: 'If You're Happy and You Know it')

There's a pat-tern in the bark of a tree. There's a pat-tern in the coat of a

bee. There are pat-terns all a-round in ev-'ry sight and ev-'ry sound, There's a

pat-tern on the skin of me. There's a pat-tern in the bricks on the wall. There's a

pat-tern in the birds' morn-ing call. There's a pat-tern in the way that

night will fol-low day, There's a pat-tern and de-sign to it all.

Hazel Priestley-Hobbs

Early years wishing well: Colours and shapes

Patterns

Personal, social and emotional development

★ Invite the children to talk about what makes bedtime special, such as having a story, or wearing cosy clean pyjamas.

★ Read books about going to bed such as *Can't You Sleep, Little Bear?* by Martin Waddell (Walker Books). Help the children to talk about any worries they have and how these might be overcome. Encourage the children to be sensitive to everyone's needs.

Communication, language and literacy

★ Turn the role-play area into a bedroom with a bed, night clothes, books, a clock and a selection of toys.

★ Show the children how to clap out the sound pattern for their names. Encourage the children to say each name as it is clapped out. Try making the rhythm with a drum, shakers and feet as well.

Mathematical development

★ Ask the children to bring in pictures which show an aspect of day or night such as sleeping, moon, stars, sun, playing outside. Use them to make two books called 'Day' and 'Night'.

★ Make biscuits and decorate them with patterns of dried fruit.

★ Build a wall using three different colours of brick. Can it be built so that no bricks of the same colour are touching?

Knowledge and understanding of the world

★ Look at the bark on different varieties of trees. Invite the children to compare the look, feel and smell of the bark and make rubbings of the different patterns.

★ Provide close-up photographs of walls in and around your setting and invite groups to match the photographs to the real thing.

★ Sit quietly outside and listen to bird-song. Follow up by asking an ornithologist to visit and explain the different song patterns of common birds.

Physical development

★ Build walls from different types of construction materials.

★ Encourage the children to develop pencil control by carefully following the handwriting patterns on the photocopiable sheet on page 96.

Creative development

★ Make bees by weaving strips of yellow paper through slots cut into ovals of black card. Finish by adding wings made from net.

★ Dance to *Flight of the Bumble Bee* (Rimsky Korsakov) pretending to be bees moving from flower to flower.

★ Make fingerprints on paper using washable-ink pads. Encourage the children to use their imagination to turn the prints into people, creatures or objects by adding detail with a fine felt-tipped pen.

Early years wishing well: Colours and shapes

The shape song

(Tune: 'Poor Jenny is a-weeping')

E   B7   E

1. I'm stand - ing in a tall shape, A tall shape, a tall shape. I'm

B7   E

stand - ing in a tall shape, I'm reach - ing up tall.

2. I'm standing in a wide shape...
I'm stretching out wide.

3. I'm sitting in a small shape...
I'm curling up small.

4. We're standing in a circle...
We're all holding hands.

5. We're crouching in a frog shape...
We're ready to jump.

6. We're sitting in a T shape...
We've all made a T.

How to use this song
Call out, for example, 'Make a wide shape on your own'. The children do this while you play once through the music. They then sing the words while standing in their shape, then wait to hear your next instruction. If you say, for example, 'Sit in a T shape all together' the whole class forms the shape of one big T. The fun here is trying to make the shape before you have played once through the music.

Alternatively, choose a child to make the shape of an animal. The others must guess what it is, then copy the shape before singing. It is advisable to try to limit the choice to a few fairly obvious shapes, such as a frog, cat, crocodile, elephant and monkey. It is fun to invent the last line of these animal verses, for example, cat – 'all cosy and warm', crocodile – 'with wide open jaws', and so on.

Ann Bryant

the shape song

Personal, social and emotional development

★ Sit in a circle holding hands. Pass a gentle squeeze from hand to hand.

★ Talk about times when we hold hands, such as when crossing the road, in new places and if we're frightened, and discuss how it can make us feel safer.

★ Provide pairs of gloves and ask each child to put on two non-matching gloves. Challenge the children to join hands in a circle so that each hand holds the hand that has the matching glove.

Communication, language and literacy

★ Chalk large letters of the alphabet onto the floor. Call out a letter for the children to find and sit on.

★ Share books about opposites with the children. Encourage them to find opposites for selected words from the song such as 'standing' and 'small'.

Mathematical development

★ Read the rhyme 'Five little Froggies Sitting on a Well' in *This Little Puffin…* compiled by Elizabeth Matterson (Puffin Books) and encourage the children to act it out by providing a tray of water, plastic frogs and interlocking bricks to make a well.

★ Invite the children to draw around their hands onto paper. Help them to cut around the outline and ask them to cover the hands with used stamps, stars or clean milk-bottle tops. Encourage the children to try to fill the space without overlapping the items. Ask them to count how many they managed to fit on their hand shape and compare the results by creating a graph.

Knowledge and understanding of the world

★ Find out about frogs: their life cycle, their habitat, how they move and what they eat.

★ Invite the children to help you collect different materials such as paper, elastic, fabric, wool, plastic and wood and find out which will stretch and which will not.

Physical development

★ Ask the children to find different ways to make a wide shape while standing, sitting, lying and moving. Join movements together to form a sequence.

Creative development

★ Encourage the children to make the shapes of different creatures. Afterwards, help the children to make up corresponding verses such as a snail 'with a shell curling round' or a butterfly 'with wings opened wide'.

★ Ask the children to roll a piece of salt dough into a sausage and then curl it up. Can they make it into an animal curling up small by adding features to their sausage body? A mouse could have a head, tail and legs added, a caterpillar just feet, and so on.

Early years wishing well: Colours and shapes

Funny food

Menu

eat and enjoy!

Puzzled beetle

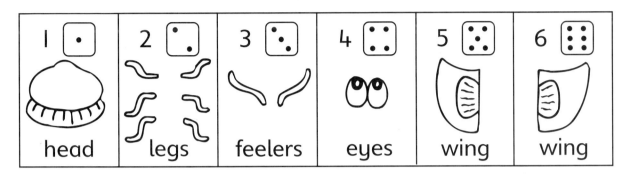

| 1 | head | 2 | legs | 3 | feelers | 4 | eyes | 5 | wing | 6 | wing |

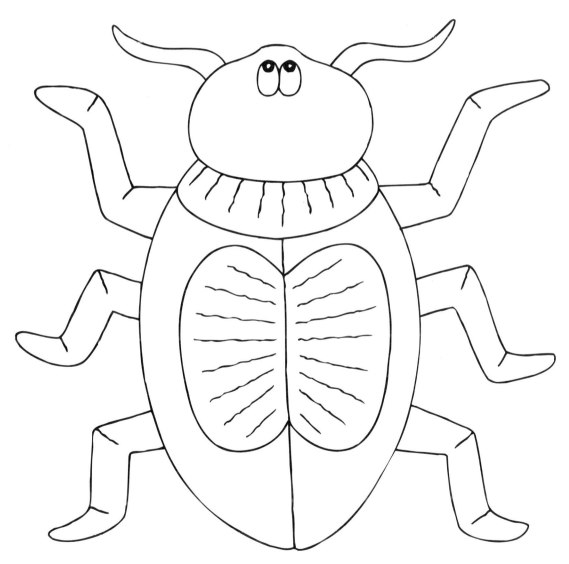

Serena's clothes

Story sequence

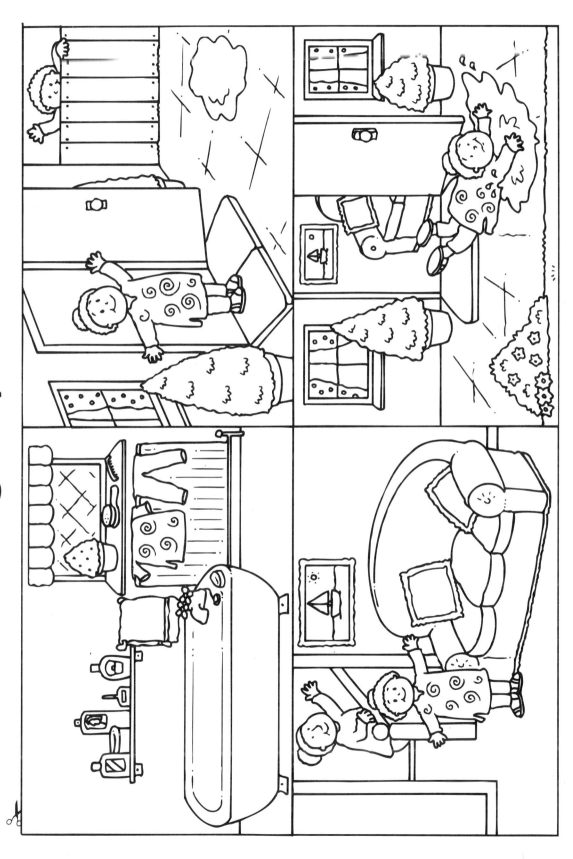

Balloon lotto

Early years wishing well: Colours and shapes

Let's go home!

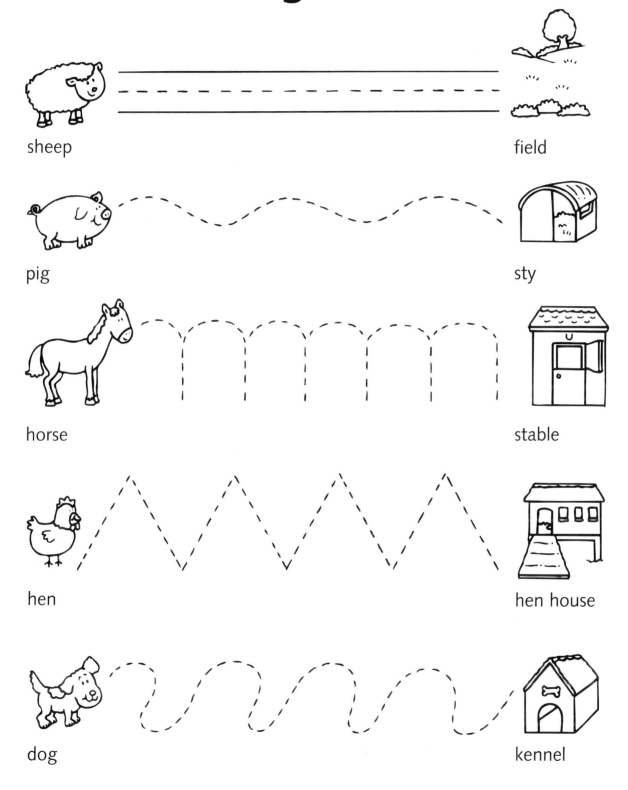

sheep   field

pig   sty

horse   stable

hen   hen house

dog   kennel

Weather chart

	Weather	Sky colour
Monday		
Tuesday		
Wednesday		
Thursday		
Friday		

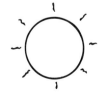  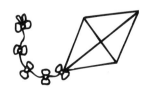

Moth template

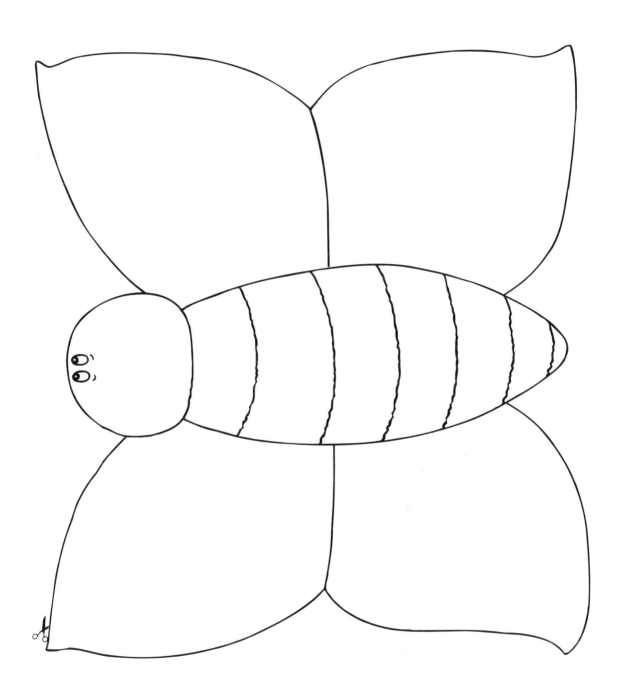

Green man, red man

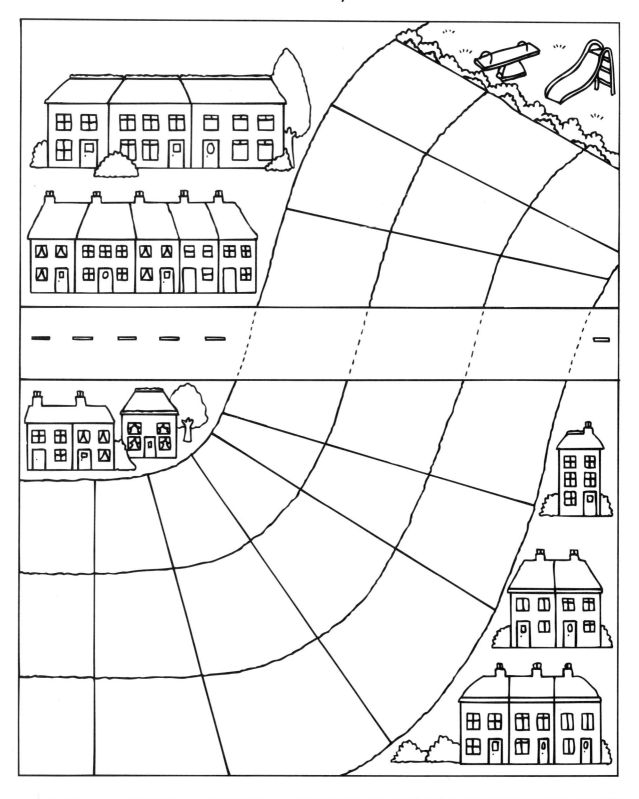

Early years wishing well: Colours and shapes

Dough shapes

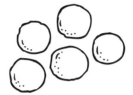

small balls

caterpillar

flower

fried egg

tower

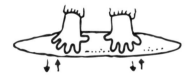

long thin worm

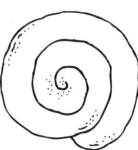

spiral snail shell

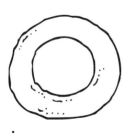

ring

fat sausage

Star puzzles

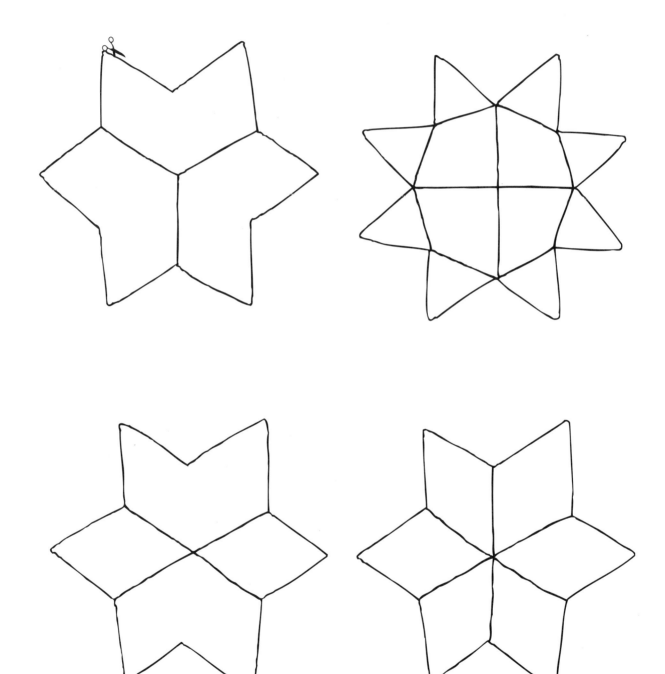

House furniture

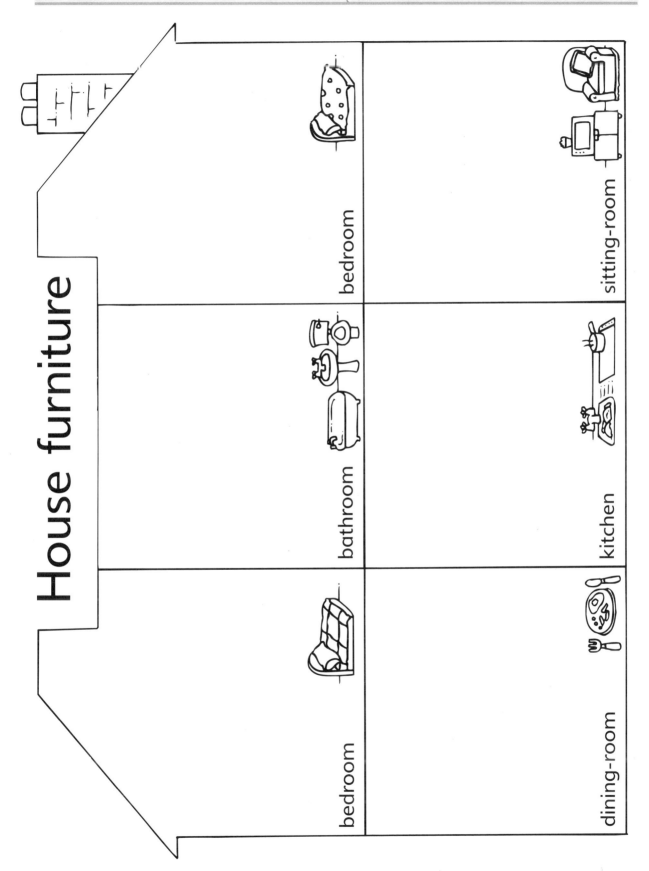

bedroom

bathroom

bedroom

sitting-room

kitchen

dining-room

Fairground jigsaws

Award badges

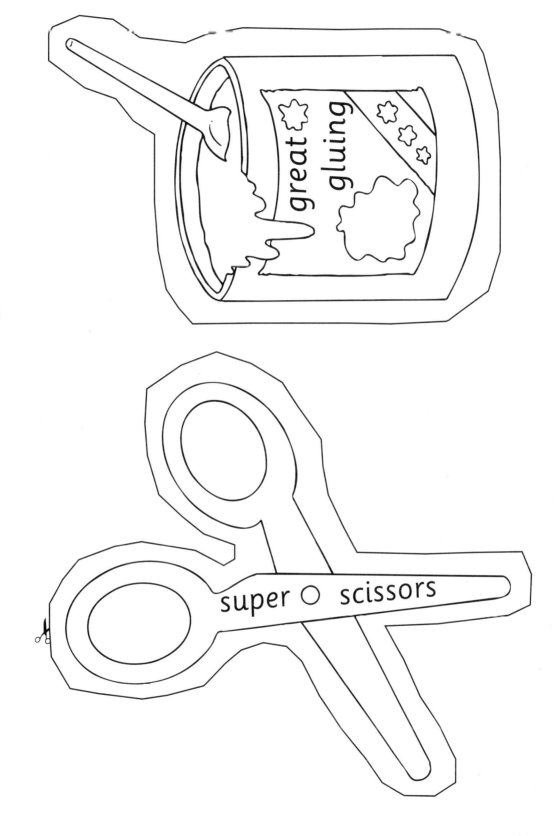

great gluing

super ○ scissors

Origami house

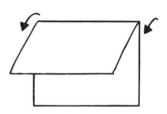

1. Fold down to here

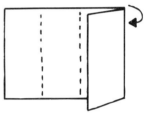

2. Crease along fold and unfold

3. Crease along to middle fold and unfold

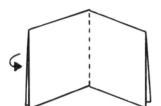

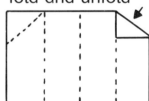

4. Crease along fold and unfold

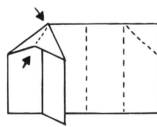

5. Push in at the large arrows and fold top layer to middle

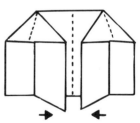

6. To make this

7. Decorate to look like a house

Symmetrical shapes

In the garden